Birds
OF
MALAWI

Birds

OF
MALAWI

A supplement to
Newman's Birds of Southern Africa

KENNETH NEWMAN
NIGEL JOHNSTON-STEWART
BOB MEDLAND

SOUTHERN
BOOK PUBLISHERS

ISBN 1 86812 418 5

First edition, first impression 1992

Published by
Southern Book Publishers (Pty) Ltd
PO Box 3103, Halfway House, 1685

Illustration by Kenneth Newman
Set in 8/9 pt Univers
by Hirt & Carter (Pty) Ltd Cape
Printed and bound by Creda Press (Pty) Ltd, Cape

CONTENTS

ACKNOWLEDGEMENTS

We wish to thank John Atkins for his generous assistance in all phases of the production of this book. In particular he spent much time and thought on the distribution maps, checklist and species accounts. Other persons without whose help gaps would have been left in the publication include Michael Dyer, who prepared lists of the birds of the Malawi national parks before he left the country in 1988; Dale Hanmer who provided her list of the birds of the Lengwe National Park; Robert Nyirenda who helped with information on the birds recorded in Liwonde National Park and Franz Karcher who made available his records from little-visited parts of Kasungu district.

Records were drawn from the Wildlife Society of Malawi magazine *Nyala*, volumes 1 to 13, and from the bulletin of ornithological news in Malawi, *Vocifer*, numbers 1 to 9. The contributors to both these publications are too numerous to acknowledge individually, but are none the less thanked and acknowledged.

We wish to specifically acknowledge the extensive use made of two books that have an important bearing on Malawi birds. *The Birds of Malawi* by C.W. and F.M.Benson, published in 1977, is full of invaluable information on the habitat and distribution of Malawi birds, and extensive use has been made of this information in the preparation of this fieldguide. Secondly we wish to thank Jo Heigham, who spent a great deal of time co-authoring *Bridging the Bird Gap*, a booklet that has led directly to the current publication.

Kenneth Newman
Nigel Johnston-Stewart
Bob Medland

INTRODUCTION

In 1982 Nigel Johnston-Stewart and Jo Heigham published a booklet on the birds of Malawi entitled *Bridging the Bird Gap*. The purpose of this publication was to describe and illustrate, for the benefit of local birdwatchers, the Malawi birds not found in regional ornithological literature available at the time. In 1982, 64 of the 630 birds recorded in Malawi were not pictured in any of the southern African field-guides.

The situation in 1992 is much the same, as *Bridging the Bird Gap* is now out of print. The number of birds recorded in Malawi is 649, of which 70 are not illustrated in recent southern African fieldguides. Two of the original *Bridging the Bird Gap* species, Basra Reed Warbler and Grey Wagtail, are now illustrated and two species, Madagascar Lesser Cuckoo and Mountain Thrush, are so similar to the already illustrated (Asian) Lesser Cuckoo and the montane race of the Olive Thrush that they do not warrant further illustrations. Three species, the Eastern (or Southern) Banded Snake Eagle, Redbreasted Wryneck and Plain Bush Warbler have been deleted from the Malawi list since 1982. In addition six species, Green Barbet, Sombre Bulbul, Yellowthroated Warbler, Barthroated Apalis, Cape Batis and Schalow's (Knysna) Lourie, have such differing plumage from the forms occurring in southern Africa that re-illustration is warranted. The number of species illustrated in this book is therefore 74.

It is intended that this book should be a companion volume to *Newman's Birds of Southern Africa* and should be used in conjunction with it.

Habitats

Brachystegia woodland is the largest and one of the most important ornithological habitats in Malawi. Although much of it has been degraded or cleared for cultivation, remains of it cover 60% to 70% of the country, with some large areas still extant. This broadleafed, open canopied deciduous woodland is found throughout at altitudes from c.500 metres on the northern and central region lake shore to over 1 800 metres on the Nyika Plateau. It is generally varied in composition with many diverse tree species occurring together. However some Brachystegia species form pure stands, for example the pure stands of *B.bussei* found at Phirilongwe. At higher altitudes Brachystegia woodland is often stunted and windswept, whereas at mid levels, if protected from fire, it attains its greatest development. Several species of birds are endemic to Brachystegia woodland, including the following which are depicted in this book: Palebilled Hornbill, Miombo Pied Barbet, Stierling's Woodpecker, Boehm's Flycatcher, Whitewinged Starling, Red and Blue Sunbird and Chestnut-mantled Sparrow-weaver.

Mopane woodland is another type of broadleafed deciduous woodland. It occurs in pure stands with few differing tree species present. In Malawi there are only small areas of this habitat, mostly to the south of Lake Malombe in Liwonde National Park and in the lower Shire valley.

In the rich fertile soils round Lilongwe at 1 100 to 1 200 metres there is a region of Acacia/Combretum woodland. Much of this habitat has unfortunately been cleared for cultivation. One of the few remaining examples is in the Lilongwe Nature Sanctuary. Savanna woodland also has Acacia trees in its very mixed composition. It is found below c.600 metres, mainly around the southern end of Lake Malawi, Lake Chilwa and throughout the upper and lower Shire valley. For the purpose of this publication these two habitats are taken together and referred to as Acacia/savanna woodland. Within this woodland are thickets, which constitute an important habitat. One of the largest remaining thicket areas is in Lengwe National Park.

Several habitats of importance are found in the montane regions that lie above c.1 500 metres. Montane evergreen forest grows in fertile, sheltered valleys, and is usually surrounded by short montane grassland. Thick tangles of bracken-brier occur on the edges of forest or in the valleys if the soils are too poor to support evergreen forest. It also establishes itself if forest is destroyed by burning or cultivation. Submontane evergreen forest grows at altitudes of c.1 200 to 1 500 metres and can cover large areas, such as at Thyolo and Mulanje.

A number of other habitats can be found at any altitude and within larger habitats. On banks of perennial streams riparian evergreen forest forms a narrow strip of vegetation where one of the commoner large trees is *Khaya nyasica*. Dambos are areas of short grass on low-lying, poorly drained soils which are waterlogged in the rainy season. Better drained areas may support long, rank grass or bracken-brier. In the vicinity of Nkhata Bay lies the only significant area of lowland evergreen forest in Malawi. Rocky mountains or outcrops are generally more common above 1 500 metres but can also be found at lower levels, such as the Nkhudzi Hills in the lake littoral.

There are many different water habitats in Malawi. Large permanent marshes with reedbeds are found along the upper reaches of the Bua River, around Lake Chilwa and at Elephant Marsh. In the dry season, when water levels fall, areas of mudflat are exposed. The principal regions of open water are Lake Chilwa and Lake Malawi, the latter being drained by the Shire River.

Species Descriptions

2

1 SHOEBILL *Balaeniceps rex.* Rare vagrant. A large, huge-billed, stork-like bird normally found in papyrus swamps. Usually solitary and secretive. There is one confirmed record for the Nyika Plateau. 110-40 cm. **M32a**

2 TUFTED DUCK *Aythya fuligula.* Rare. A palaearctic summer vagrant. A small, dark duck with tufted head, blue-grey bill and yellow eyes; white to off-white flank panels, belly and wing feathers conspicuous in the male only when in breeding plumage; the male in eclipse plumage is duller while the female is generally plain brown above. Known from one old record from northern Lake Malawi. 43 cm. **M52**

3 COMMON (EUROPEAN) SNIPE *Gallinago gallinago.* Rare. A palaearctic summer vagrant recorded once in the northern region. Difficult to distinguish from the resident African (Ethiopian) Snipe *G.nigripennis* but paler upperparts and distinctive chestnut tail pattern, *lacking white outer tail feathers*, are diagnostic. Flushes with a zig-zag action and utters a harsh 'creech'. Like all snipes it feeds in marshy ground and on edges of floodlands. 27 cm. **M172**

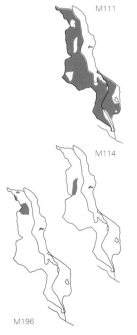

M111

4 HILDEBRANDT'S FRANCOLIN *Francolinus hildebrandti.* Fairly common and widespread resident. Both sexes have a red bill and red legs with spurs, the male with conspicuously marked underparts. The female illustrated is of the northern race; females of the southern race have the nape, hind neck and chest uniform with the upperparts. The call is a loud, three-noted 'kok-kok-kok' repeated and becoming louder and higher. Found in small coveys in dense bush, bracken-brier thickets and in rank growth in rocky hills. 35-8 cm. **M111**

M114

5 SCALY FRANCOLIN *Francolinus squamatus.* Rare localised resident. Only the male has spurs, sexes otherwise alike. Has a guttural two-note call. Occurs on the Viphya Plateau between 900 and 1 800 metres in evergreen forest and adjacent bracken-brier. 25-31 cm. **M114**

6 PINKBREASTED TURTLE DOVE *Streptopelia lugens.* Uncommon localised resident. A dark grey to sooty-brown dove with darker lateral neck patches; female less pink on breast, immature without neck patches. The call is a deep, four-note 'coo, cooo, coo, coo' the second syllable longer and higher pitched. Occurs in or on the fringes of high altitude evergreen forest, often foraging in small flocks on the ground or in tree tops. 28 cm. **M196**

M196

1 Shoebill

2 ♂ ♀ Tufted Duck

3 Common (European) Snipe

5 Scaly Francolin

4 ♂ ♀ Hildebrandt's Francolin

6 Pinkbreasted Turtle Dove

4

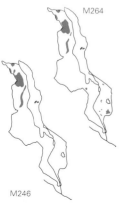

1 BLACKFACED LOURIE *Corythaixoides personata*. Uncommon, localised resident. The bare face and chin and distinctive colouring make this lourie unmistakable; sexes alike. The voice is a loud 'ko-arr, ko-arr'. Confined to the Chitipa district where it occurs on wooded termitaria or in riparian evergreen forest. 51 cm. **M214**

2 SCHALOW'S LOURIE *Tauraco schalowi*. Common resident. Differs from the similar Livingstone's Lourie *(T. livingstoni)* mainly in having a longer crest and a much harsher, slower call. Occurs in the mid-stratum and canopy of evergreen and riparian forest and in Brachystegia woodland west of the Rift from Tambali northwards. 47 cm. **M211**

3 PALEBILLED HORNBILL *Tockus pallidirostris*. Uncommon resident. Similar to the Grey Hornbill *T.nasutus* but has paler, heavier bill and lacks the pure white underparts of that species. The piping call is similar to that of the Grey Hornbill but of higher pitch. Occurs in dry bush and Brachystegia woodland between 500 and 1 500 metres. 43-6 cm. **M292**

4 BARTAILED TROGON *Apaloderma vittatum*. Fairly common resident. Similar to the Narina Trogon *A.narina* but has the silvery under-tail feathers barred black. The call is a quiet mewing 'phee-ew, phee-ew' plus a loud 'kow, kow, kow'. Found in montane and submontane evergreen forests between 1 400 and 2 100 metres where it either hawks insects or sits motionless for long periods. 30 cm. **M264**

5 MOUNTAIN NIGHTJAR *Caprimulgus poliocephalus*. Fairly common resident. In the field told from other nightjars only with difficulty but in the hand shows white spots (buff in the female) on first four primary feathers: cf. Freckled Nightjar *C.tristigma*. Best identified by call; a shrill 'tiree-tireeee' the last syllable wavering. Occurs in montane and submontane fringes of evergreen forests and adjacent grasslands from the Viphya Plateau northwards. 24 cm. **M246**

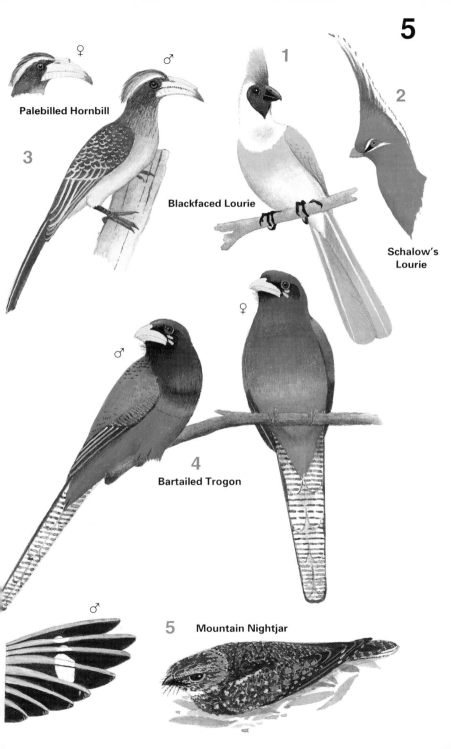

5

Palebilled Hornbill

♀

♂

1

Blackfaced Lourie

2

3

Schalow's
Lourie

♂

♀

4

Bartailed Trogon

♂

5   Mountain Nightjar

6

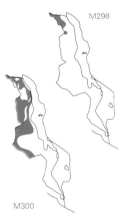

1 GREEN BARBET *Buccanodon olivaceum*. Common localised resident. Differs from the related Woodward's Barbet *Cryptolybia woodwardii* of Zululand in being blacker about the head and upper breast. Race A *B.o.belcheri* (Thyolo Mountain) lacks yellow ear coverts, while race B *B.o.rungweensis* (Misuku Hills) is less black about the head and upper breast. The call, by which it is usually first detected, is a loud 'chop chop chop'. Occurs in pairs, small parties or mixed bird parties in the mid-stratum and canopy of submontane evergreen forest. 14,5-17,5 cm. **M302**

2 MOUSTACHED GREEN TINKERBIRD *Pogoniulus leucomystax*. Common resident. A small, dull green barbet with a whitish moustachial streak, yellow rump and yellow edges to wing and tail feathers. The identifying call is a continuing, monotonous 'chuga chug chug chuga chug chug' plus an occasional shrill trill. Frequents the canopy of montane and submontane evergreen forest, often in mixed bird parties. 10,5 cm. **M304**

3 BLACKBACKED BARBET *Lybius minor*. Uncommon localised resident. Distinguished by black upperparts (except for red forehead) with a white V on the mantle; bill whitish. Sexes alike. The call is a quiet 'tonk tonk'. Occurs from the foothills of the Nyika Plateau northwards at 1 200 and 1 500 metres where pairs and small groups congregate in the canopy of riparian evergreen forest. A quiet barbet, seldom mixing with other birds. 18 cm. **M298**

4 MIOMBO PIED BARBET *Lybius frontatus*. Uncommon, localised resident. Differs from the larger Pied Barbet *L. leucomelas* in lacking the black mask and throat-patch and having heavily spotted underparts. The call is a deep 'poop poop poop . . .' repeated up to 18 times, plus a harsh double note 'ki-aaa' repeated five or six times. Found in Brachystegia woodland up to 1 650 metres where pairs join mixed bird parties, probing the bark for insects. 14,5 cm. **M300**

5 BROWNBREASTED BARBET *Lybius melanopterus*. Uncommon localised resident. Red forehead, face and throat plus brown and white underparts distinctive. Sexes alike. Makes a harsh nasal 'aark-aark'. Found within thickets in the Liwonde National Park and possibly also further north near the lake shore at Makanjila and Karonga. Pairs and small family parties frequent low bushes and the canopy. 20 cm. **M297**

6 STIERLING'S WOODPECKER *Dendropicos stierlingi*. Uncommon localised resident. Differs from the similar Cardinal Woodpecker *D.fuscescens* in having the mantle and wings unmarked, the male with black, the female with brown ear coverts. The call is a shrill chittering; pairs also maintain contact with a low churring sound. Has a limited distribution at 1 000 to 1 300 metres in Brachystegia woodland where it joins mixed bird parties while feeding in any part of the tree. 15-15,5 cm. **M320**

M302

M304

M298

M300

M297

M320

7

Green Barbet — 1

Moustached Green Tinkerbird — 2

Blackbacked Barbet — 3

Miombo Pied Barbet — 4

Brownbreasted Barbet — 5

Stierling's Woodpecker — 6

8

1 REDRUMPED SWALLOW *Hirundo daurica.* Locally common resident. Differs from other similar swallows in the blue cap being virtually separated from the mantle by a chestnut collar; the under wing coverts are pale rufous, the tail all dark. The contact call is a soft 'djuit', the song a pleasant twittering ending in a trill. Occurs in small flocks above 1 200 metres where it hawks insects with other swallows or swifts. 16-17 cm. **M342**

2 WHITEHEADED SAW-WING SWALLOW *Psalidoprocne albiceps.* Fairly common summer resident. The male is characterised by a conspicuous white head, the female, with white throat only best told from swifts by flight style (see below). Usually silent but sometimes makes a weak twittering. Frequents the edges of evergreen forest and Brachystegia woodland above 1 200 metres but will also forage in open country. Flies slowly and hesitantly at low altitude, normally in small groups. 13 cm. **M349**

3 MOUNTAIN BABBLER *Alcippe abyssinica.* Uncommon localised resident. Head, neck and cheeks dark blue-grey, the crown nape and throat streaked black, mantle to tail warm olive-brown breast to belly grey blotched white, flanks and belly olive-brown sexes alike. Immature has crown and nape as rest of upperparts throat whitish, no black streaking. Groups make a continual twittering while feeding and individual males utter a tuneful song from the forest canopy morning and evening. Small groups feed in the ground stratum of montane and submontane evergreen forest 13 cm. **M365**

4 MOUNTAIN ILLADOPSIS *Malacocinchla pyrrhoptera.* Rare localised resident. Identified by dark olivaceous upperparts and belly, rest of underparts pale grey; sexes alike. Voice not documented. Occurs in small parties in dense undergrowth of montane evergreen forest at 2 000 to 2 300 metres. A little known species 14 cm. **M366**

9

1 Redrumped Swallow

2 Whiteheaded Saw-wing Swallow

Imm.

3 Mountain Babbler

Mountain Illadopsis

4

10

M330

1 FISCHER'S FINCHLARK *Eremopterix leucopareia*. Uncommon localised resident. The male differs from similar sparrow-like larks in having a chestnut crown-patch and hind collar plus whiter flanks; the female probably inseparable in the field from others. Birds in a flock call a low 'tweet-ees'. Found in widely separated localities, occurring in small flocks in dry, short grassland from Mchinji northwards. 12 cm. **M330**

2 WHITE WAGTAIL *Motacilla alba*. Rare summer palaearctic vagrant. Differs from African Pied Wagtail *M.aguimp* in being more white about the head (non-breeding plumage), black only on central crown and nape. The call is a typical wagtail 'chissik'. Habitat and behaviour much like that of African Pied Wagtail. Known only from two old records from Mangochi. 18 cm. **M504**

M508

3 WOOD PIPIT *Anthus nyassae*. Common resident within its restricted habitat. Similar to the extralimital Longbilled Pipit *A.similis* but shorter billed and shorter tailed, the hind neck greyish-brown, rest of upperparts more ochraceous red-brown, eyebrow white, chin white, rest of underparts deeper buffy, the breast well streaked. Sexes alike. Voice not documented but probably similar to that of *A.similis*. Found only in Brachystegia woodland where it feeds on the ground but perches in trees. 17 cm. **M508**

M508a

4 JACKSON'S PIPIT *Anthus latistriatus*. (A recently acknowledged species.) Fairly common resident. Differs from the previous species in being darker on the upperparts, the feather centres being blackish-brown, feather edges less straw-coloured, hind neck not visibly paler than rest, underparts more heavily marked the streaking extending to the flanks. Voice not documented Normally occurs in montane summit grasslands above the tree line, living among rocks and grass tufts, but undergoes a post breeding movement to lower altitudes. 17 cm. **M508a**

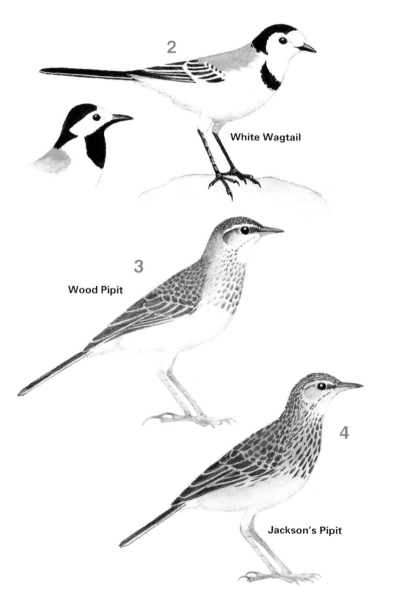

11

Fischer's Finchlark

White Wagtail

Wood Pipit

Jackson's Pipit

12

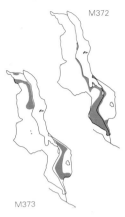

M372

M373

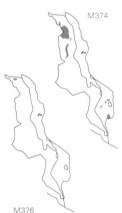

1 SOMBRE BULBUL *Andropadus importunus*. Common resident. The Malawi race of this common bulbul differs from the nominate race in being brighter green on the upperparts and more yellowish on the underparts. The well-known call of the species is often shortened to 'prrit cheri cheri'. Secretive in dense bush and thickets at lower altitudes where it is heard more often than seen. 24 cm. **M372**

2 LITTLE GREEN BULBUL *Andropadus virens*. Fairly common resident. Upperparts dark olive-green, underparts lighter olive-green, tail washed brown; eye dark, bill stubby, black with *distinctive orange gape*. The call is 'werk werk werk, widdly widdly widdly widdly weee' rising in scale. Sings for long periods and is more often heard than seen. Inhabitats the mid-stratum of riparian and submontane evergreen forest. 16,5 cm. **M373**

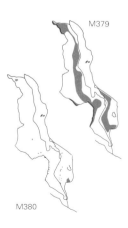

M374

M376

M379

M380

3 OLIVEBREASTED MOUNTAIN BULBUL (GREENBUL) *Andropadus tephrolaemus*. Common resident. Distinguished by dark blue-grey head, neck and upper breast, olive-green wings and tail and *white eye-lids*; sexes alike. Calls a much repeated 'chip, chop, jueee'. Occurs in mixed bird parties on the fringes of montane evergreen forest, usually above 1 800 metres. Individuals move to lower altitudes when not breeding. A noisy and obtrusive bird 21 cm. **M374**

4 MONTANE BULBUL (SHELLEY'S GREENBUL) *Andropadus montanus*. Fairly common resident in its restricted range. A small, sombrely coloured bulbul, entirely olive-green, but paler on underparts, particularly on throat. Sexes alike. Generally silent but has a soft call. Found only in evergreen montane forest in the Misuku Hills above 1 200 metres. Forages in the mid-stratum. 17 cm **M376**

5 GREY-OLIVE BULBUL (GREENBUL) *Phyllastrephus cerviniventris*. Fairly common resident. Differs from the similar Terrestrial Bulbul *P.terrestris* in having the rump and tail chestnut-brown and the chest and belly buffy. Groups are noisy when foraging, calling 'kwa kwa kwa kwee kwee kwee'. Occurs in riparian and submontane forest where it feeds on the ground. 18 cm. **M379**

6 PLACID BULBUL (FISCHER'S GREENBUL) *Phyllastrephus placidus*. Fairly common resident. Upperparts dark olive-brown, tail dull brown, underparts whitish faintly streaked pale yellow; the eye with a thin whitish orbital ring. Sexes alike. The call is 'trrip trrip trrip trrip'. Small groups are found in the ground stratum of montane and submontane evergreen forest. A tame species which flicks its wings as it searches the forest floor, often in the vicinity of red ants. 19 cm. **M380**

13

1 Sombre Bulbul

2 Little Green Bulbul

3 Olivebreasted Mountain Bulbul

4 Montane Bulbul

5 Grey-olive Bulbul

6 Placid Bulbul

14

M392

1 CENTRAL BEARDED SCRUB ROBIN *Erythropygia barbata*
Fairly common resident. Differs from the (Eastern) Bearded Robin
E.quadrivirgata mainly in being greyer on nape and mantle, whiter
below and pale orange only on upper breast and flanks, otherwise
closely similar. The song is a striking crescendo of loud and clear
notes with local variations. Usually singly or in pairs on bush-cov-
ered termitaria within Brachystegia woodland at between 1 000
and 1 500 metres. 17 cm. **M392**

2 RUFOUS BUSHCHAT *Erythropygia galactotes*. Rare palaearctic
summer vagrant. A small robin-chat with dark brown upperparts
(eastern European race), whitish underparts and a conspicuous
rufous tail that is frequently raised and fanned. The call is a hard
'tek tek'; its song is probably not heard in Africa. Recorded only
once: in the Shire valley in Acacia woodland and thickets. 15 cm.
M390b

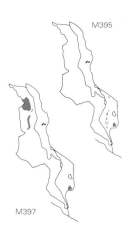

M395

M397

3 CHOLO ALETHE *Alethe choloensis*. Fairly common but localised resident. Differs from the similar Whitebreasted Alethe
A.fuelleborni in being more olive-brown above, the tail white-
tipped, throat white, rest of underparts pale olive-brown, flanks
grey. The immature is dull cream below blotched tawny. Calls
before the rains, a repetitive 'tui eee' and similar tuneless whistles.
Inhabits the ground stratum of submontane evergreen forest at
800 to 1 200 metres, often feeding in the vicinity of red ants with
other ant-following species. 18-21 cm. **M395**

4 OLIVEFLANKED ROBIN *Alethe anomala*. Fairly common localised resident. Two races. In the northern race *A.a.macclounii* (as
illustrated) the upperparts are olivaceous-grey merging to darker on
the crown and the white eyebrow is distinct; in the nominate race
A.a.anomala, found only on Mulanje Mountain, the upperparts are
olive-brown, the eyebrow off-white and reduced. Sexes alike. The
call is a two-tone 'eee oo ooee', the alarm call a deep 'harr'.
Inhabits the ground stratum of montane evergreen forest. Shy and
retiring. 15 cm. **M397**

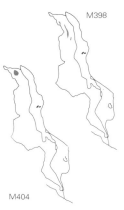

M398

M404

5 SHARPE'S AKALAT *Sheppardia sharpei*. Uncommon localised
resident. Above entirely dark olivaceous-brown, eyebrow inconspicuous pale grey, spot in front of eye white, below chin to upper
breast pale chestnut, breast and flanks olivaceous brown, belly
white. Sexes alike. Has a brief, weak song 'tt-tt-tuiddy'. Inhabits
the ground stratum of evergreen forest at 1 800 to 2 100 metres. A
quiet, retiring species and easily overlooked. 13 cm. **M398**

6 SPOT-THROAT MODULATRIX *Modulatrix stictigula*. Rare localised resident. Above dark olivaceous-brown, the tail with a chestnut wash; below throat buffy white spotted black, rest of underparts rich chestnut-brown, belly white. The distinctive call is a
plaintive, drawn-out whistle with almost a rattle in the middle; also
has a beautiful thrush-like song. Known only from evergreen forest
at Matipa and Wilindi in the Misuku Hills of the far north. Shy and
secretive, frequenting the ground stratum. 16 cm. **M404**

15

Central Bearded Scrub Robin 1

Rufous Bushchat 2

Cholo Alethe 3

Oliveflanked Robin 4

Spot-throat Modulatrix 6

Sharpe's Akalat 5

16

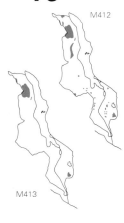

1 EASTERN FOREST SCRUB WARBLER (EVERGREEN FOREST WARBLER) *Bradypterus mariae*. Common resident. Has dark brown upperparts; crown and chin white, eyebrow creamy, tail shorter than the next species and with a frayed appearance, underparts buffy with an olive-brown wash over the breast and flanks, throat and belly whitish. Sexes alike; immature washed yellow on the underparts. The call, sometimes given by a pair in duet, is a rapid rattling, 'tiku-tiku-tiku-tik' and a chirping 'chep-chep'. Inhabits dense undergrowth in evergreen forest above 1 300 metres. Like others in its genus tame and inquisitive but extremely difficult to see as it clambers about in tangled thickets. 13 cm. **M412**

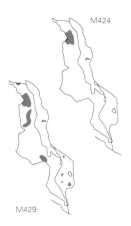

2 LONGTAILED FOREST SCRUB WARBLER (CINNAMON BRACKEN WARBLER) *Bradypterus cinnamomeus*. Common localised resident. Similar in appearance to the previous species but is reddish-brown above and has a longer tail. Sexes alike; immature washed yellow on underparts. The call is a high-pitched 'hi-chwi-chwi-chwi...' in a long sequence. Pairs occur in dense tangles in bracken-brier and other dense herbage on Mulanje Mountain and mountains near the Nyika Plateau. 14 cm. **M413**

3 YELLOW MOUNTAIN WARBLER *Chloropeta similis*. Fairly common localised resident. Differs from the (African) Yellow Warbler *C.natalensis* in being slightly smaller and having green (not brown) upperparts; sexes alike. The immature is washed buff. Has a short musical song. Frequents bracken-brier and rank grass along drainage lines above 2 000 metres. Normally secretive but occasionally perches conspicuously; frequently raises its crown feathers. 13 cm. **M424**

4 EUROPEAN BLACKCAP *Sylvia atricapilla*. Rare palaearctic summer visitor. Both sexes distinctive: male mainly ashy-grey above with black cap; cheeks, throat and breast grey; female differs in being browner above with a chestnut cap. Prior to its return migration sings a high-pitched and varied song reminiscent of a Garden Warbler *Sylvia borin*. In Malawi has been recorded mainly on the edges of evergreen forest above 1 000 metres. 14 cm. **M429**

5 BROWN WARBLER (BROWN PARISOMA) *Parisoma lugens*. Uncommon localised resident. Identified by dark brown upperparts, blackish lores, *outer tail feathers tipped and edged white* and smoky-white underparts with chin and throat mottled black. Sexes alike. Calls a rapid 'ta-ta-ta-ta...' up to eight times and has a short, musical song. Occurs only around Dedza and on the Nyika Plateau where it forages for insects in the canopies of Mountain Acacia *Acacia abyssinica*. 15 cm. **M431**

6 EUROPEAN BARRED WARBLER *Sylvia nisoria*. Rare palaearctic summer vagrant. Yellow eye and well-barred underparts diagnostic of male; female and immature have less barring. Has a warbling song given in short bursts. Known only by two records from the lower Shire valley where found in sparse Acacia woodland. 15 cm. **M430a**

17

1 **Eastern Forest Scrub Warbler**

2 **Longtailed Forest Scrub Warbler**

3 **Yellow Mountain Warbler**

4 ♀ ♂ **European Blackcap**

5 **Brown Warbler**

6 ♂ **European Barred Warbler**

18

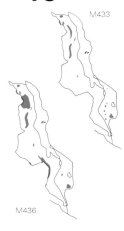

1 YELLOWTHROATED WARBLER *Seicercus ruficapillus*. Fairly common resident. Differs from the southern race mainly in having a grey (not yellow) breast; only throat and vent yellow. Sexes alike. Call and behaviour as for the southern race. Found in the mid-stratum of evergreen montane and submontane forest. 11 cm. **M433**

2 BARTHROATED APALIS *Apalis thoracica*. Common resident. In Malawi three distinct races: *A.t.youngi* (not illustrated) similar to (c) on p.341 of *Newman's Birds of Southern Africa; A.t.whitei* (a) east of the Rift has grey crown, olive-green mantle and the underparts entirely deep yellow with olive-green flanks, a black mask from bill to ear coverts contiguous with throat-bar; *A.t.murina* (b) to the north of the Nyika Plateau has a dark brown cap to below the eye (no mask), grey mantle and white underparts washed pale yellow from belly to vent. Call and behaviour as for other races. Inhabits the fringes of montane and submontane evergreen forest and bracken-brier. 12-13 cm. **M436**

3 WHITEWINGED APALIS *Apalis chariessa*. Uncommon localised resident. Long, graduated tail and bright colouring unmistakable; the male with black upperparts, female with grey cap, wings and tail and green back. The call is a loud 'twitawit twitawit twitawit'. Pairs frequent the canopy and mid-stratum of submontane and riparian evergreen forest. Lively birds, often in mixed bird parties. 15 cm. **M437**

4 CHESTNUT-THROATED APALIS *Apalis porphyrolaema*. Fairly common resident. Forehead, sides of face, throat and breast rich chestnut-brown, back grey, graduated tail dark brown with paler feather-tips, belly to vent creamy-white. Calls 'chi chi chi'. Found in the canopy and mid-stratum of montane and submontane evergreen forest from Chirobwe northwards. 13 cm. **M439**

5 BROWNHEADED APALIS *Apalis cinerea*. Uncommon localised resident. Entire cap brown, lores black, rest of upperparts grey, underparts creamy-white, the flanks washed grey. Normally calls a high-pitched 'trrr-tik-tik-tik'. An active leaf gleaner found in the canopy and mid-stratum of evergreen forest above 1 500 metres in the far north. 13 cm. **M440**

19

1 Yellowthroated Warbler

2 **a**

b

Barthroated Apalis

♂

3 Whitewinged Apalis ♀

4

Chestnut-throated Apalis

5

Brownheaded Apalis

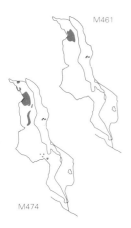

1 TRILLING CISTICOLA *Cisticola woosnami.* Uncommon localised resident. Similar to the northern race of the Neddicky *C.fulvicapilla*, the male with upperparts from nape to tail duskier brown, including ear coverts; female smaller and more lightly coloured. The call is diagnostic, a soft reeling, slightly crescendic trill lasting up to five seconds. The male adopts a tree-top perch and calls for long periods, moving its head from side to side. Found in short grass and low bushes within Brachystegia woodland. When disturbed remains in the grass uttering hard churring sounds. 13 cm. **M455**

2 MOUNTAIN CISTICOLA (BLACKLORED CISTICOLA) *Cisticola hunteri.* Fairly common localised resident. Distinguished from other local cisticolas by its large size and blackish lores. Sexes alike, female smaller. The call is reminiscent of the sound made by a rusty wheel; male and female often sing in duet from prominent perches with tails fanned. Inhabits tall rank grass and bracken-brier above 2 250 metres. 15 cm. **M456**

3 CHURRING CISTICOLA *Cisticola njombe.* Fairly common localised resident. Similar to Wailing Cisticola *C.lais.* Best identified by call and behaviour. A noisy species, the song a repetitive 'churr-churr-churr' from a prominent perch; while moving about within cover makes a soft churring sound. Found on the Nyika Plateau above 2 000 metres in long grass and bracken-brier. The tail is usually held cocked. 12 cm. **M461**

4 SLATY FLYCATCHER *Melaenornis chocolatina.* Fairly common resident. A fairly large flycatcher, the entire upperparts dark blue-slate, distinct white eye-ring, chin and belly whitish, breast and flanks dusky. Sexes alike. Generally quiet but may make a loud 'zit' plus a descending chatter. Found in the canopy and edges of montane and riparian evergreen forest, from Dedza northwards above 1 500 metres, where it hawks insects from a perch. 17 cm. **M474**

5 BOEHM'S FLYCATCHER *Myopornis boehmi.* Fairly common resident. Has same dumpy appearance and behaviour as Dusky Flycatcher *Muscicapa adusta.* This species has the brown upperparts streaked black, wing feathers edged pale buff, white lores and eye-ring, and white underparts with blackish arrow-like spots across the breast and flanks, only throat and belly unmarked. Calls 'chee chip' or 'zee ee chip'. Found in Brachystegia woodland where it hawks flying insects from a perch. 11,5 cm. **M472**

6 WHITETAILED BLUE FLYCATCHER *Elminia albicauda.* Fairly common resident. This beautiful little bird is unmistakable. Sexes alike. The call is 'chirrup see ee'. Occurs on the edges of riparian evergreen forest and Bachystegia woodland between 1 000 and 1 200 metres. Lively and highly active, darting out after insects and stiffly fanning its wings and tail. 14 cm. **M484**

21

1 Trilling Cisticola

2 Mountain Cisticola

3 Churring Cisticola

4 Slaty Flycatcher

5 Boehm's Flycatcher

6 Whitetailed Blue Flycatcher

22

M478

1 CAPE BATIS *Batis capensis*. Common resident. Males differ from those of the southern race in lacking chestnut colouring entirely, wing coverts, primary edges and flanks white. Calls and behaviour as for the nominate race. Inhabits montane and submontane evergreen forest. 12-13 cm. **M478**

2 REDTAILED SHRIKE (ISABELLINE SHRIKE) *Lanius isabellinus*. Rare palaearctic summer vagrant. Differs from the Redbacked Shrike *L.collurio* in being buffy on crown and mantle; rump bright chestnut, tail deep reddish-brown, belly and flanks pale buff. Voice and behaviour as in Redbacked Shrike. Recorded in the far north. 16 cm. **M514a**

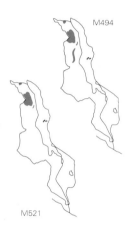

M494

3 FÜLLEBORN'S BLACK BOUBOU *Laniarius fuelleborni*. Fairly common localised resident. An entirely dark slaty-black boubou shrike; sexes closely similar. A common call is a loud 'kweek kweek' plus a variety of ringing, liquid calls given in duet. Frequents the ground stratum of montane and submontane evergreen forest where pairs are more easily heard than seen. 19 cm. **M494**

4 WALLER'S REDWINGED STARLING *Onychognathus walleri*. Fairly common localised resident. In both sexes the tail has a cut-off appearance; plumage of male glossy blue-black with a purple sheen to the crown and breast; the female with head and breast greyish. The voice is a variety of whistles and chatters. Usually seen in noisy groups of up to 30 birds flying above the canopy of montane evergreen forest. 25-7 cm. **M521**

M521

5 SLENDERBILLED REDWINGED STARLING *Onychognathus tenuirostris*. Uncommon localised resident. Both sexes have slender bills and the central tail feathers elongated; the male's plumage glossy blue-black with green and violet sheens, the female with grey-tipped head and breast feathers. Utters shrill whistles and chattering notes. Recorded on the Nyika and Viphya Plateaux where flocks feed at forest edges, forest clearings (not in forest) and in the vicinity of waterfalls. 25 cm. **M523**

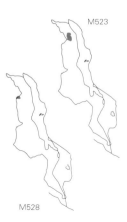

M523

6 WHITEWINGED BABBLING STARLING *Neocichla gutturalis*. Uncommon localised resident. The striking colouring of this starling renders it unmistakable. Utters a variety of continuous, high-pitched chittering and grating notes. Occurs in flocks in Brachystegia woodland in the Rumphi district adjoining Zambia. The behaviour is unstarling-like, the flight heavy, more akin to that of a babbler or helmet-shrike. 20 cm. **M528**

M528

23

1 ♀ ♂

Cape Batis

Redtailed Shrike

2

3

Fülleborn's
Black Boubou

♀

4

♂

5 ♂ ♀

♂

Waller's
Redwinged Starling

Slenderbilled
Redwinged Starling

Whitewinged
Babbling Starling

6

24

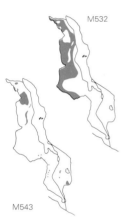

1 REDTUFTED MALACHITE SUNBIRD *Nectarinia johnstoni*. Uncommon localised resident. The metallic blue-green male with its long tail is unmistakable; the red pectoral tufts can be inconspicuous in both sexes. Has a variety of calls including a continuous 'chi chi chi chi...'. Found on the Nyika Plateau and Mafinga Mountains where it feeds on proteas and ericas. 13-30 cm. **M548**

2 GREENHEADED SUNBIRD *Nectarinia verticalis*. Uncommon resident. In both sexes the crown and ear coverts are metallic green, rest of upperparts olive-green, the underparts grey; the male has a metallic blue chin, throat and breast plus cream-coloured pectoral tufts. The call is a strident double note; also has a soft warbling song. Occurs in riparian evergreen forest and on the edges of montane and submontane evergreen forest. 14 cm. **M536**

3 RED AND BLUE SUNBIRD (ANCHIETA'S SUNBIRD) *Anthreptes anchietae*. Common resident. In this brightly coloured sunbird both sexes are unmistakable, though the female is duller. The call is 'tee', often repeated; also has a weak warbling song. Occurs in the canopy of Brachystegia woodland, often in mixed bird parties. 10 cm. **M532**

4 EASTERN DOUBLECOLLARED SUNBIRD *Nectarinia mediocris*. Common resident. Though smaller this species is distinguished from other doublecollared sunbirds by its bright olive-green belly and by habitat. Frequently utters a clear, sharp 'tssp tssp tssp'. Normally occurs above 1 500 metres where it inhabits bracken-brier or the mid-stratum and edges of evergreen forest, descending to lower altitudes in winter. 10 cm. **M543**

5 OUSTALET'S SUNBIRD *Nectarinia oustaleti*. Uncommon localised resident. Male told from male Whitebellied Sunbird *N. talatala* by more greenish colouring of the head, mantle and breast, a broad band of purplish-maroon across the lower breast and shorter, straighter bill; the pectoral tufts are yellow or orange. Female, apart from shorter bill, is very similar to female Whitebellied Sunbird. Utters a double or single 'tsik' in flight, the male with a typical sunbird song. Occurs in degraded Brachystegia woodland. 11,5 cm. **M539a**

♂

Oustalet's Sunbird

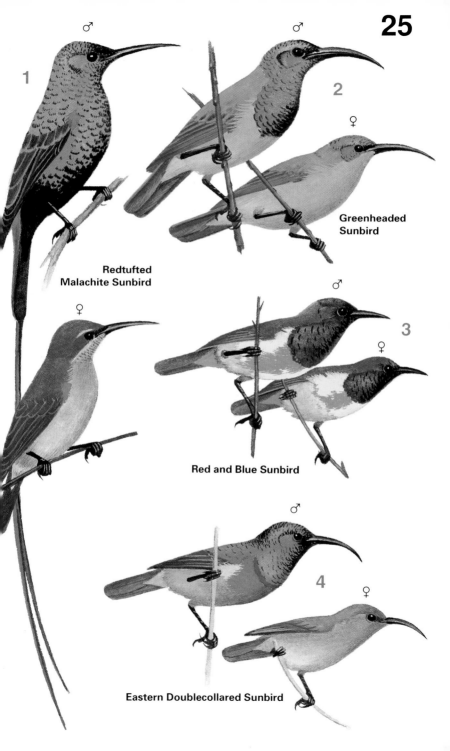

25

♂

1

♂

2

♀

Greenheaded Sunbird

Redtufted Malachite Sunbird

♀

♂

3

♀

Red and Blue Sunbird

♂

4

♀

Eastern Doublecollared Sunbird

26

1 MOUNTAIN MARSH WIDOW *Euplectes psammocromius.* Common localised resident. In breeding plumage the male is distinctive; in non-breeding plumage it resembles the female but is larger and retains the yellow shoulder. Voice similar to other *Euplectes* species. Confined to upland valleys on the Nyika Plateau. In the non-breeding season often in large flocks. MM 35 cm. FF 14 cm. **M572**

2 BAGLAFECHT WEAVER *Ploceus baglafecht.* Uncommon localised resident. Male has the entire head from base of lower mandible to hind neck black, breast yellow and belly pale buffy, the eye pale yellow; female closely similar but has the crown mixed green and black. Voice not documented. A solitary, insectivorous weaver, in Malawi confined to the Nyika Plateau where it frequents the edges of montane evergreen forest and dense vegetation in river valleys. 15 cm. **M552**

3 BERTRAM'S WEAVER *Ploceus bertrandi.* Uncommon resident. Male distinguished by saffron crown and forehead, black patch on nape and black mask extending to the throat, female with entirely black head, both sexes with pale yellow eyes and *olive-green upperparts from mantle to tail.* Makes a sparrow-like chirp and has a brief chattering song. Pairs and family groups are widely but sparsely distributed in riverine evergreen forest, bracken-brier or rank grass at 1 200 to 1 500 metres. Sometimes breeds in gardens in the Blantyre district. 15 cm. **M553**

4 CARDINAL QUELEA *Quelea cardinalis.* Rare occasional resident. Male differs from the male Redheaded Quelea *Q.erythrops* in having the red of the head extending to the breast but not to the nape, the chin red (not blackish); female probably indistinguishable unless with male, but is smaller and more compact than the female Redheaded Quelea. Flocks make a twittering sound. Has bred few times in long rank grass near Lilongwe, otherwise unknown in Malawi. 13 cm. **M564**

5 CHESTNUTMANTLED SPARROW-WEAVER *Plocepasser rufocapulatus.* Uncommon localised resident. Differs from Whitebrowed Sparrow-weaver *P.mahali* in head markings, whitish bill and rich chestnut mantle; sexes alike but female has a blackish bill. Call not documented. Small groups of up to 15 birds feed on the ground in Brachystegia woodland from the northern end of Kasungu National Park to Vwaza Marsh. Tame and lethargic. 18 cm. **M577**

♀ Mountain Marsh Widow

1 ♂

♂ Baglafecht Weaver 2

♂ Bertram's Weaver 3 ♀

♂ Cardinal Quelea 4 ♀

Chestnutmantled Sparrow-weaver 5

28

1 CRIMSONRUMPED WAXBILL *Estrilda rhodopyga.* Uncommon localised resident. Differs from the Common Waxbill *E.astrild* in having a black (not red) bill plus red rump and wing markings. Sexes alike. Inhabits dry scrub and old cultivations on the northern shore of Lake Malawi and Likoma Island. Small groups search for seeds on the ground much like other waxbills. 10 cm. **M599**

2 AFRICAN CITRIL *Serinus citrinelloides.* Common resident. Male may or may not have the black mask, sexes otherwise similar. The call is a series of rising, discordant whistles. Pairs and small groups occur in rank grass in Brachystegia woodland, bracken-brier and also in gardens at 1 000 to 1 800 metres. 11,5 cm. **M616**

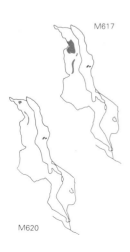

3 STRIPEBREASTED CANARY (SEEDEATER) *Serinus reichardi* Common resident. Very similar to the Streakyheaded Canary *S.gularis* but has whiter underparts and streaking on breast and flanks. Sexes alike. The call is a quiet 'see-seee'. Occurs in the Mangochi Forest region and Kirk Range northwards at 1 000 to 1 800 metres. Feeds near the ground and in the canopy of Brachystegia woodland. 14 cm. **M618**

4 STREAKY CANARY (SEEDEATER) *Serinus striolatus.* Fairly common localised resident. The only streaky, brown canary with yellow eyebrow and upper breast. Sexes alike. Has a typical canary song and a high-pitched 'seep-seep-seep-seep-seep' call. Found in upland valleys above 2 000 metres where small groups feed in bracken-brier and in other dense vegetation. 15 cm. **M617**

5 ORIOLE FINCH *Linurgus olivaceus.* Rare localised resident. Male distinctive with black head, yellow body and orange bill; female mostly olive-green with orange bill. Usually silent, sometimes uttering a soft 'tsssp'. Feeds on the ground in small flocks near the edge of montane evergreen forest. 13 cm. **M620**

1 Crimsonrumped Waxbill

2 ♀ ♂ African Citril

3 Stripebreasted Canary

4 Streaky Canary

5 ♂ ♀ Oriole Finch

MAP 1
ALTITUDE

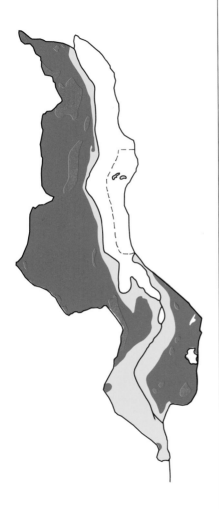

- above 1 500 m
- 600 m to 1 500 m
- below 600 m

MAP 2
REGIONS and NATIONAL PARKS

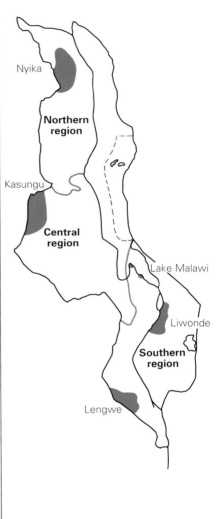

Nyika

Northern region

Kasungu

Central region

Lake Malawi

Liwonde

Southern region

Lengwe

- National Parks
- Borders

MAP 3
LOCALITIES

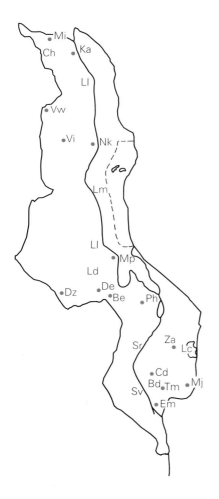

Common to all regions
Ll Lake Malawi littoral
Lm Lake Malawi

Northern region
Ch Chitipa district
Mi Misuku Hills F.R.
Ka Karonga
Vw Vwaza Marsh G.R.
Nk Nkwadzi F.R. (Chinteche)
Vi Viphya Plateau F.R.

Central region
Mp Mpatsanjoka Dambo
Ld Lilongwe district
Dz Dzalanyama F.R.
De Dedza F.R.
Be Bembeke Dambo (Dedza)

Southern region
Ph Phirilongwe F.R.
Za Zomba Plateau F.R.
Lc Lake Chilwa
Cd Chileka Dambo
Bd Blantyre district
Tm Thyolo Mountain F.R.
Mj Mulanje Mountain F.R.
Sv Shire valley
Sr Shire River
Em Elephant Marsh

MAP 4
HABITATS

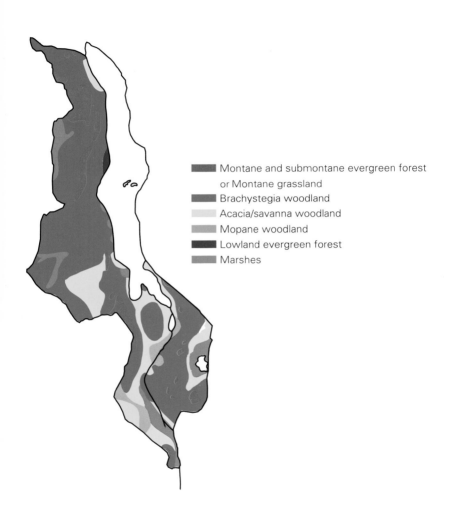

■ Montane and submontane evergreen forest
  or Montane grassland
■ Brachystegia woodland
□ Acacia/savanna woodland
■ Mopane woodland
■ Lowland evergreen forest
■ Marshes

ABBREVIATIONS USED IN CHECKLIST

In order to fit the annotated checklist into the space available it has been necessary to make use of a number of abbreviations. An explanation of these abbreviations is given below.

BOM: Malawi bird number. These numbers correspond with the numbers on the new Malawi bird species record card and *The Birds of Malawi*, C.W. and F.M. Benson, 1977. All species new to Malawi are given an 'A' suffix and placed in the appropriate scientific order.

Family/Species: The English and scientific nomenclature is from *Newman's Birds of Southern Africa*, K.B. Newman, 1991.

Stat: Status:
R   Rare, a species recorded 10 times or less in any year in suitable habitat.
U   Uncommon, a species recorded 30 times or less a month in suitable habitat.
F   Fairly common, a species recorded 1-10 times a day in suitable habitat.
C   Common, a species recorded 10-50 times a day in suitable habitat.
V   Very common, a species recorded 50-100 times a day in suitable habitat.
A   Abundant, a species recorded 100 times or more a day in suitable habitat.
W   Winter, April to August.
S   Summer, September to March.
L   Localised, a species seen only in restricted areas of suitable habitat.
Re   Resident, a species that breeds in Malawi.
Vi   Visitor, a non-breeding species (palaearctic, Malagasy or intra-Africa migrant)
Va   Vagrant, a species not normally seen in Malawi.

Note: Readers used to the ornithological terminology in common use in Malawi should note the different interpretation of a resident and visitor (migrant) used in this book. For example Wahlberg's Eagle is considered an intra-Africa migrant in Malawi as it is not present throughout the year. In this book it is termed a summer resident as it breeds in the country.

Al: Altitude:
See Map 1
H   High, above 1 500 m
M   Mid, 600-1 500 m
L   Low, below 600 m
A   All altitudes

Note: The altitudes given here are meant as a general indication of usual altitudinal range. Some birds do wander or infrequently visit abnormal altitudes on passage. An example of this is the Cinnamon Roller which occasionally visits the Nyika Plateau above 2 000 m, but is normally found at mid to low levels.

Ra: Range: N   Northern region of Malawi
See Map 2   C   Central region
               S   Southern region
               T   Throughout the country

Note: The boundaries of the various regions of Malawi are not clearly delineated.

National Parks: N   Nyika
See Map 2   K   Kasungu
               Li Liwonde
               L   Lengwe

Note: Records from the new Lake Malawi National Park are not listed here as it has not been in existence for long and information is too scanty. This area was proclaimed a national park to protect the endemic Lake Malawi fish.

Local: Localities: Name abbreviations of localities where certain birds may be
See Map 3   found, if this is not obvious from the national park lists.

Ll	Lake Malawi littoral	Common to all regions
Lm	Lake Malawi	
Ch	Chitipa district	. Northern region
Mi	Misuku Hills F.R.	
Ka	Karonga	
Vw	Vwaza Marsh G.R.	
Nk	Nkwadzi F.R. (Chinteche)	
Vi	Viphya Plateau F.R.	
Mp	Mpatsanjoka Dambo (Salima)	Central region
Ld	Lilongwe district	
Dz	Dzalanyama F.R.	
De	Dedza F.R.	
Be	Bembeke Dambo (Dedza)	
Ph	Phirilongwe F.R.	Southern region
Za	Zomba Plateau F.R.	
Lc	Lake Chilwa	
Cd	Chileka Dambo	
Bd	Blantyre district	
Tm	Thyolo Mountain F.R.	
Mj	Mulanje Mountain F.R.	
Sv	Shire valley	
Sr	Shire River	
Em	Elephant Marsh	

Habitat: Br Brachystegia woodland (Miombo)
See Map 4   Mo Mopane woodland
             Ac Acacia/savanna woodland
             Th Thicket
             Ro Rocky mountains, hills or outcrops
             Ef Evergreen forest, type will be specified in the comments column.

Bb   Bracken and brier
Gl   Grass, long or rank
Gs   Grassland, short
Dw Dambo, wet or seasonally wet short grass
Ma Marshes, light vegetation, aquatic plants or reeds giving partial cover to the water surface
Ow Open water, lakes, lagoons, dams, sewage works, etc
Mf   Mudflats, sandbars or beaches
Ri   Rivers, large or small, rocky, banks usually wooded
*   Four or more habitats

Note: A brief description of the various habitats is given in the introduction.

Comments: A cross reference (e.g. ***See page 11***) in bold italic to where the bird is described and illustrated in this volume follows any comments in this column. For each bird not described in this book, its page reference in *Newman's Birds of Southern Africa* is given in **bold** type.

ANNOTATED CHECKLIST

BOM	Family / species	Stat.	Al.	Ra.	Nat. Park
	Grebes PODICIPEDIDAE				
1	Dabchick *Tachybaptus ruficollis*	C/Re	A	T	N K – L
	Pelicans PELECANIDAE				
2	White Pelican *Pelecanus onocrolatus*	U/RE	ML	T	N – – L
3	Pinkbacked Pelican *P. rufescens*	F/Re	ML	T	– K Li L
	Cormorants PHALACROCORACIDAE				
4	Whitebreasted Cormorant *Phalacrocorax carbo*	A/Re	ML	T	– – Li –
5	Reed Cormorant *P. africanus*	A/Re	ML	T	N K Li –
	Darters ANHINGIDAE				
6	Darter *Anhinga melanogaster*	C/Re	ML	T	– K Li –
	Herons and egrets ARDEIDAE				
7	Bittern *Botaurus stellaris*	RLRe	M	S	– – – –
8	Little Bittern *Ixobrychus minutus*	U/Re	ML	T	– – Li –
9	Dwarf Bittern *I. sturmii*	U/Re	ML	T	– – Li L
10	Blackcrowned Night Heron *Nycticorax nycticorax*	F/Re	ML	T	– K Li L
11	Whitebacked Night Heron *Gorsachius leuconotus*	RLRe	ML	T	– – Li –
12	Squacco Heron *Ardeola ralloides*	A/Re	ML	T	N K Li L
12A	Madagascar Squacco Heron *A. idae*	RWVi	ML	CS	– – – –
13	Cattle Egret *Bubulcus ibis*	A/Re	A	T	N K Li L
14	Greenbacked Heron *Butorides striatus*	F/Re	ML	T	– K Li –
15	Rufousbellied Heron *B. rufiventris*	U/Re	ML	T	– K Li –
16	Black Egret *Egretta ardesiaca*	C/Re	ML	T	– K Li –
17	Great White Egret *E. alba*	C/Re	ML	T	N K Li –

Local.	Habitat	Comments
Mp, Em	Ma, Ow	Prefers water with some cover; soon colonises new dams. **p. 96**
Lc, Em	Ma, Ow	Regular only on Lake Chilwa and Elephant Marsh. **p. 62**
Mp, Em	Ma, Ow	Local movements. Pelican spp. have even been seen flying over Mulanje Mountain. **p. 62**
Lm	Ma, Ow	Uncommon on small areas of water. **p. 64**
	Ma, Ow, Ri	Occurs in any water habitat, including small dams. **p. 64**
Mp, Em	Ma, Ow, Ri	Not common on Lake Malawi. **p. 64**
Lc, Cd	Ma	The only sight record is from the Chileka Dambo. **p. 70**
Sr, Em	Ma	Palaearctic migrant and resident birds in summer. **p. 66**
Lc, Sr	Dw, Ri	Skulks in woody vegetation bordering its habitat. **p. 66**
Ld, Bd	Ri, Ow	Water usually tree lined. **p 70**
Ld, Sr	Ri, Ow	Water likely to be heavily wooded; regularly seen at Discovery Lodge. **p. 70**
Mp, Em	*	Any water or marsh habitat. **p. 68**
Mp, Bd	Ma, Ow	May be regular, but easily confused with the previous species. **p. 68**
	*	**p. 72**
Mp, Em	Ma, Ri	Often in reeds and trees on the fringes of its habitat. **p. 66**
Mp	Ma	Regular only around Salima. **p. 66**
Mp, Em	Ma	**p. 68**
Mp, Em	Ma	**p. 72**

BOM	Family / species	Stat.	Al.	Ra.	Nat. Park
18	Yellowbilled Egret *E. intermedia*	F/Re	ML	T	N K Li L
19	Little Egret *E. garzetta*	V/Re	ML	T	N K Li –
20	Grey Heron *Ardea cinerea*	V/Re	ML	T	– K Li –
21	Blackheaded Heron *A. melanocephala*	C/Re	A	T	N K Li L
22	Goliath Heron *A. goliath*	F/Re	ML	T	– K Li –
23	Purple Heron *A. purpurea*	F/Re	ML	T	– K Li –
24	**Hamerkop** SCOPIDAE Hamerkop *Scopus umbretta*	A/Re	ML	T	N K Li L
25	**Storks** CICONIIDAE White Stork *Ciconia ciconia*	FSVi	A	T	N K Li L
26	Black Stork *C. nigra*	U/Re	ML	T	N K Li –
27	Abdim's Stork *C. abdimii*	USVi	A	T	N K Li L
28	Woollynecked Stork *C. episcopus*	U/Re	ML	T	– K Li L
29	Saddlebilled Stork *Ephippiorhynchus senegalensis*	ULRe	ML	T	– K Li L
30	Openbilled Stork *Anastomus lamelligerus*	A/Re	ML	T	N K Li L
31	Marabou Stork *Leptoptilos crumeniferus*	U/Re	ML	T	– K Li L
32	Yellowbilled Stork *Mycteria ibis*	F/Re	ML	T	N K Li –
32A	**Shoebill** BALAENICIPITIDAE Shoebill *Balaeniceps rex*	R/Va	H	N	N – – –
33	**Ibises and spoonbills** PLATALEIDAE Sacred Ibis *Threskiornis aethiopicus*	F/Re	ML	T	– K Li –
34	Hadeda Ibis *Bostrychia hagedash*	F/Re	ML	T	N K Li L
35	Glossy Ibis *Plegadis falcinellus*	V/Re	ML	T	N K Li L
36	African Spoonbill *Platalea alba*	U/Re	ML	T	N K Li –

Local.	Habitat	Comments
Mp, Em	Ma	Least common of the four white egrets. **p. 72**
Mp, Em	Ma	**p. 72**
	*	Occurs in any water habitat. **p. 74**
	*	Prefers drier situations than the previous species. **p. 74**
Mp, Em	Ma	**p. 74**
Mp, Em	Ma	**p. 74**
	*	**p. 80**
Be, Bd	Gs, Dw	Regular in large numbers at the Thuchila Farm Institute and all dambos in the central region. **p 78**
Dz, Ll	Ro	Chongoni F.R.; breeds on rocky hills, feeds in other habitats. **p. 78**
De, Cd	Gs, Dw	**p. 78**
Mp	Ma, Ri	Often at the main hide waterhole in Lengwe N.P. **p 80**
Vw	Gs	Infrequently seen outside protected areas nowadays. **p. 76**
Mp, Em	Ma, Ow	Often soars on thermals far from water. **p. 80**
Ll,Em	*	Appears quite common around the western shore of Lake Malombe. **p. 76**
Mp, Em	Ma, Ow	**p. 80**
	Ma	*See page 2.*
Mp, Em	Ma	**p. 84**
Mp, Sr	Ma, Ri	Common at Mvuu Camp in Liwonde N.P. **p. 84**
Mp, Em	Ma	By far the commonest ibis. **p. 84**
Mp, Em	Ma	**p. 82**

BOM	Family / species	Stat.	Al.	Ra.	Nat. Park
	Flamingos PHOENICOPTERIDAE				
37	Greater Flamingo *Phoenicopterus ruber*	USVi	ML	T	N K Li –
38	Lesser Flamingo *P. minor*	RWVi	M	S	– – Li –
	Ducks and geese ANATIDAE				
39	Fulvous Duck *Dendrocygna bicolor*	V/Re	ML	T	– K Li –
40	Whitefaced Duck *D. viduata*	A/Re	ML	T	– K Li L
41	Egyptian Goose *Alopochen aegyptiacus*	ULRe	ML	T	– K Li –
42	Spurwinged Goose *Plectropterus gambensis*	C/Re	ML	T	– K Li L
43	Knobbilled Duck *Sarkidiornis melanotos*	C/Re	ML	T	N K Li L
44	Pygmy Goose *Nettapus auritus*	F/Re	ML	T	– – Li –
45	African Black Duck *Anas sparsa*	F/Re	HM	T	N K – –
45A	Cape Teal *A. capensis*	RWVa	M	C	– – – –
46	Yellowbilled Duck *A. undulata*	C/Re	HM	T	N K Li –
46A	Pintail *A. acuta*	RSVi	L	C	– – – –
47	Redbilled Teal *A. erythrorhyncha*	C/Re	ML	T	N K Li –
48	Hottentot Teal *A. hottentota*	C/Re	ML	T	– K Li –
49	Garganey *A. querquedula*	USVi	ML	T	– – – –
50	European Shoveller *A. clypeata*	RSVi	ML	N	– – – –
51	Southern Pochard *Netta erythrophthalma*	F/Re	ML	T	N K Li –
52	Tufted Duck *Aythya fuligula*	RSVi	L	N	– – – –
52A	Maccoa Duck *Oxyura maccoa*	RSVa	H	N	N – – –
53	Whitebacked Duck *Thalassornis leuconotus*	U/Re	ML	T	– – Li –

Local.	Habitat	Comments
Lm, Em	Ma, Ow	**p. 82**
Lm, Sr	Ow	Much less common than the previous species. **p. 82**
Mp, Em	Ma, Ow	**p. 86**
Vw, Em	Ma, Ow	**p. 86**
Vw, Sr	Ri, Ow	Common in Vwaza Marsh Game Reserve. **p. 88**
Vw, Em	Ma	**p. 88**
Vw, Em	Ma	**p. 94**
Lc, Em	Ma	Fairly common where there are lily pads. **p. 88**
Za, Mj	Ri, Ow	Prefers heavily shaded rocky rivers or streams. **p. 94**
Ld	Ow	Recorded once only at Bunda Dam, occurrence elsewhere possible. **p. 92**
Vw, Be	Ma	Uncommon east of the Rift, but one of the commonest ducks in the central and northern regions. **p. 94**
Mp	Ma	Recorded twice at Mpatsanjoka Dambo, occurrence elsewhere possible in the Lake Malawi littoral and Shire valley. **p. 94**
Vw, Em	Ma	**p. 90**
Mp, Em	Ma	**p. 90**
Mp, Em	Ma	Regular in small numbers at the Kasinthula Fish Ponds near Chikwawa. **p. 92**
Ka, Lm	Ow	Known from two pre-1977 records in the Lake Malawi littoral. **p. 92**
Mp, Em	Ma	**p. 90**
Ka	Ma	*See page 2.*
	Ow	Two records to date, both from dams on the Nyika Plateau. **p. 90**
Mp, Em	Ma, Ow	Regular in the Elephant Marsh and Kuti Pond, Salima; scarce elsewhere. **p. 86**

BOM	Family / species	Stat.	Al.	Ra.	Nat. Park
	Secretarybird SAGITTARIIDAE				
54	Secretarybird *Sagittarius serpentarius*	RLRe	HM	T	N K – –
	Vultures, harriers, eagles, hawks, etc. ACCIPITRIDAE				
55	Lappetfaced Vulture *Torgos tracheliotus*	U/Re	A	T	N K Li L
56	Whiteheaded Vulture *Trigonoceps occipitalis*	U/Re	A	T	N K Li L
57	Whitebacked Vulture *Gyps africanus*	F/Re	A	T	N K Li L
58	Hooded Vulture *Necrosyrtes monachus*	U/Re	ML	T	N K Li L
59	Palmnut Vulture *Gypohierax angolensis*	U/Re	ML	T	N K Li L
60	Pallid Harrier *Circus macrourus*	FSVi	HM	T	N K – –
61	Montagu's Harrier *C. pygargus*	USVi	A	T	N – Li L
62	African Marsh Harrier *C. ranivorus*	C/Re	ML	T	N K Li –
62A	European Marsh Harrier *C. aeruginosus*	RSVi	HM	T	N – – –
63	Gymnogene *Polyboroides typus*	F/Re	ML	T	N K Li L
64	Bateleur *Terathropius ecaudatus*	F/Re	ML	T	N K Li L
65	Blackbreasted Snake Eagle *Circaetus gallicus*	C/Re	ML	T	N K Li L
66	Brown Snake Eagle *C. cinereus*	C/Re	ML	T	N K Li L
67	Western Banded Snake Eagle *C. cinerascens*	F/Re	ML	T	N K Li L
68	Black Sparrowhawk *Accipiter melanoleucus*	C/Re	A	T	N – Li L
69	Redbreasted Sparrowhawk *A. rufiventris*	U/Re	H	N	N – – –
70	Ovambo Sparrowhawk *A. ovampensis*	U/Re	ML	T	– K – L
71	African Goshawk *A. tachiro*	F/Re	A	T	N – Li L
72	Little Banded Goshawk *A. badius*	C/Re	ML	T	N K Li L
73	Little Sparrowhawk *A. minullus*	U/Re	ML	T	– K Li L

Local.	Habitat	Comments
	Gs	Only vagrants occur outside Nyika and Kasungu N.P. **p. 150**
	*	Vultures are not common in Malawi outside the national parks and this is the least common species. **p. 154**
	*	**p. 154**
	*	The commonest Malawi vulture. **p. 152**
	*	**p. 154**
Mj	*	Feeds on seeds of Raffia palms. **p. 156**
Vi	Gs	Uncommon except on the Nyika Plateau. Summer only. **p. 182**
Lc	Gs	**p. 182**
Mp, Em	Dw, Ma	**p. 182**
Ld, Lc	Dw, Ma	Difficult to tell in the field from the previous species and much less common. Summer only. **p. 180**
Mj, Sv	*	**p. 184**
Ll, Sv	*	Common in the lower Shire valley and Lake Malawi littoral. **p. 160**
	*	Prefers open country, grassland and aerodromes. **p.160**
	*	Generally in low, drier areas but in the central region also common higher. **p. 160**
Ld, Sv	*	Very common in the lower Shire valley. **p. 158**
Mj	Br, Ef	Nests in riparian evergreen forest and bluegum plantations. **p. 180**
Vi	Bb, Gs	Common only on the Nyika Plateau; hunts along roads. **p. 174**
Ch	Br, Ac	**p. 176**
Vi, Mj	Br, Ef	Associated with all types of evergreen forest, where it breeds. **p. 178**
	Br, Mo, Ac	**p. 176**
Bd	Br, Ac, Th	Prefers richer woodland than the previous species, including riparian evergreen forest. **p. 176**

BOM	Family / species	Stat.	Al.	Ra.	Nat. Park
74	Dark Chanting Goshawk *Melierax metabates*	U/Re	ML	T	N K Li L
75	Gabar Goshawk *Micronisus gabar*	F/Re	ML	T	– K Li L
76	Lizard Buzzard *Kaupifalco monogrammicus*	V/Re	ML	T	N K Li L
77	Augur Buzzard *Buteo augur*	C/Re	HM	T	N – Li –
78	Steppe Buzzard *B. buteo*	ASVi	A	T	N K Li L
78A	Forest Buzzard *B. oreophilus*	RLRe	H	T	N – – –
79	Longcrested Eagle *Lophaetus occipitalis*	F/Re	ML	T	N K Li L
80	Crowned Eagle *Stephanoaetus coronatus*	F/Re	A	T	N K Li L
81	Martial Eagle *Polemaetus bellicosus*	F/Re	ML	T	N K Li L
82	African Hawk Eagle *Hieraaetus fasciatus*	F/Re	ML	T	N K Li L
83	Booted Eagle *H. pennatus*	USVi	A	T	N K – L
84	Ayres' Eagle *H. ayresii*	U/Re	M	T	N – – L
85	Black Eagle *Aquila verrauxii*	ULRe	HM	T	N – Li –
86	Tawny Eagle *A. rapax*	UWVi	HM	T	N – – L
87	Steppe Eagle *A. nipalensis*	USVi	A	T	N K – L
88	Lesser Spotted Eagle *A. pomarina*	FSVi	A	T	N K Li L
89	Wahlberg's Eagle *A. wahlbergi*	VSRe	ML	T	N K Li L
90	African Fish Eagle *Haliaeetus vocifer*	V/Re	ML	T	N K Li L
91	Yellowbilled Kite *Milvus migrans*	A/Re	A	T	N K Li L
92	Honey Buzzard *Pernis apivorus*	USVi	A	T	N – – L
93	Cuckoo Hawk *Aviceda cuculoides*	U/Re	NK	T	N K – –
94	Blackshouldered Kite *Elanus caeruleus*	F/Re	A	T	N K Li L

Local.	Habitat	Comments
Ld, Za	Br, Ac	Not common east of the Rift. **p. 178**
Ll, Sv	Ac	Generally in drier areas than the Little Banded Goshawk. **p. 176**
	Br, Mo, Ac	**p. 174**
	Ro	Most often around rocky hills or mountains, but wanders in other habitats. **p. 172**
	*	**p. 170**
Mi	*	Known only from the Nyika Plateau and the Misuku Hills. **p. 170**
Bd, Mj	Br, Mo, Ac	**p. 164**
De, Mj	Ef, Th, Ro	Breeds in submontane and montane evergreen forest. **p. 166**
Ld, Ll	Br, Ac	Found in more open areas than the previous species. **p. 168**
Ll, Mj	Br, Ac, Ro	**p. 166**
Ld, Lc	*	**p. 162**
Ll, Mj	Br, Ro	**p. 166**
Ll, Mj	Ro	Restricted to rocky hills and mountains. **p. 168**
Ld	*	Not uncommon in Lilongwe district during the dry season. **p. 164**
Sv, Mj	*	**p. 164**
Vi, Mj	*	The commonest large palaearctic eagle. Summer only. **p. 162**
	Br, Mo, Ac	Breeds in Brachystegia and Acacia woodland. Present in summer, a few individuals arrive earlier. **p. 162**
Lm	Ma, Ow, Ri	Any water habitat. **p. 168**
	*	Present July to March; the Black Kite although much less common also occurs in Malawi on passage. **p. 158**
Lc, Mj	Br, Ac	Even seen in riparian evergreen forest on Zomba Plateau. **p. 172**
Ph, Bd	Br	**p. 186**
	Br, Gs	Hunts over areas with short grass and scattered trees and is attracted to sugar plantations at Dwangwa and Nchalo. **p. 174**

BOM	Family / species	Stat.	Al.	Ra.	Nat. Park
95	Bat Hawk *Macheiramphus alcinus*	U/Re	ML	T	N K – –
96	**Osprey** PANDIONIDAE Osprey *Pandion haliaetus*	Vi	ML	T	N K Li –
97	**Falcons and kestrels** FALCONIDAE Lanner Falcon *Falco biarmicus*	C/Re	A	T	N K Li L
98	Peregrine Falcon *F. peregrinus*	ULRe	A	T	N K Li –
99	Taita Falcon *F. fasciinucha*	RLRe	M	CS	– – – –
99A	African Hobby Falcon *F. cuvierii*	R/Re	M	CS	– – Li –
100	Hobby Falcon *F. subbuteo*	CSVi	A	T	N K Li L
100A	Sooty Falcon *F. concolor*	RSVi	ML	S	– – – –
101	Rednecked Falcon *F. chicquera*	ULRe	ML	T	– – Li L
102	Dickinson's Kestrel *F. dickinsoni*	C/Re	ML	T	N K Li L
103	Western Redfooted Kestrel (Falcon) *F. vespertinus*	RSVi	HM	T	N – – –
104	Eastern Redfooted Kestrel (Falcon) *P. amurensis*	FSVi	A	T	N K Li –
105	Lesser Kestrel *F. naumanni*	USVi	A	T	N K Li –
106	Rock Kestrel *F. tinnunculus*	F/Re	A	T	N – – –
106A	Grey Kestrel *F. ardosiaceus*	R/Va	L	N	– – – –
107	**Francolins and quails** PHASIANIDAE Coqui Francolin *Francolinus coqui*	U/Re	M	NC	N K – –
108	Crested Francolin *F. sephaena*	ULRe	L	S	– – Li L
109	Shelley's Francolin *F. shelleyi*	U/Re	HM	T	N K – –
110	Redwing Francolin *F. levaillantii*	FLRe	H	N	N – – –
111	Hildebrandt's Francolin *F. hildebrandti*	F/Re	A	T	N – – –

Local.	Habitat	Comments
Bd	Br, Mo, Ac	Only likely to be seen at dusk when bats emerge. **p. 184**
Mp, Sr	Ma, Ow, Ri	Fairly common on the upper Shire River. **p. 184**
	Ro	Frequents small rocky hills but wanders into other habitats. **p. 188**
De, Mj	Ro	Fairly common on Mulanje Mountain. **p. 188**
	Ro	Known only from near Neno, associated with cliffs. **p. 186**
Ld	Ac	Recent records from near Lilongwe and in Liwonde N.P. **p. 190**
	*	**p. 188**
Lc, Sv	Ac	Only six records to date from Liwonde N.P., Lake Chilwa and the lower Shire valley. **p. 186**
Ka, Em	Ac	Feeds and breeds near Borassus palms. **p. 186**
	Ac	Breeds in Borassus or Hyphaene palms. **p. 190**
Ld, Bd	*	Much less common than the next species. **p. 192**
De, Bd	*	Attracted to hatches of flying termites, sometimes in large numbers. **p. 192**
Bd, Em	*	Mainly over grassland or open country. **p. 192**
Mj	Ro	Common on small rocky hills. **p. 192**
Ka	*	Known from one specimen collected in 1989 near Karonga. **p. 190**
Dz, Za	Br	Generally in dry areas of Brachystegia woodland. **p. 142**
Sv	Th	Found in thicket from Mangochi southwards in the Rift Valley. **p. 142**
Mj, Za	Bb, Gs	Fairly common in montane grassland, bracken and brier above 1 500 m. **p. 146**
	Gs	Confined to the Nyika Plateau. **p. 146**
De, Mj	Ef, Th, Bb	***See page 2.***

BOM	Family / species	Stat.	Al.	Ra.	Nat. Park
112	Rednecked Francolin *F. afer*	V/Re	A	T	N K Li L
113	Swainson's Francolin *F. swainsonii*	RLRe	M	N	– – – –
114	Scaly Francolin *F. squamatus*	ULRe	HM	N	– – – –
115	Common Quail *Coturnix coturnix*	U/Re	HM	T	N – – –
116	Harlequin Quail *C. delegorguei*	USRe	ML	T	N K – L
117	Blue Quail *C. adansonii*	U/Re	ML	T	N – – –
	Guineafowls NUMIDIDAE				
118	Helmeted Guineafowl *Numida meleagris*	V/Re	ML	T	N K Li L
119	Crested Guineafowl *Guttera pucherani*	ULRe	L	NS	– – – L
	Buttonquails TURNICIDAE				
120	Kurrichane Buttonquail *Turnix sylvatica*	F/Re	ML	T	N K – L
121	Blackrumped Buttonquail *T. hottentotta*	U/Re	M	S	– – – –
	Cranes GRUIDAE				
122	Wattled Crane *Grus carunculata*	RLRe	HM	NC	N K – –
123	Crowned Crane *Balearica regulorum*	U/Re	ML	NC	N K – –
	Rails, crakes, flufftails, etc. RALLIDAE				
124	African Rail *Rallus caerulescens*	U/Re	ML	T	– K Li –
125	Corncrake *Crex crex*	USVi	A	T	– – – –
126	African Crake *C. egregia*	USRe	ML	T	– K – L
127	Baillon's Crake *Porzana pusilla*	R/Re	M	S	– – – –
128	Spotted Crake *P. porzana*	RSVi	M	T	– – – –
129	Striped Crake *Aenigmatolimnas marginalis*	RSRe	ML	T	– – – –

Local.	Habitat	Comments
	*	**p. 144**
Vw	Mo	No recent records. **p. 144**
Vi	Ef, Bb	*See page 2.*
De, Mj	Gs, Dw	Fairly common in areas of montane grassland. **p. 140**
Ld, Sv	Gl	Little known but probably occurs in much thicker vegetation than the next species. Present in summer only. **p. 140**
Vi, Sv	Gs, Dw	Rarely alongside the Harlequin Quail. **p. 140**
	*	**p. 148**
Nk, Sv	Ef, Th	May also survive in lowland evergreen forest in the Malawi Hills and Nkwadzi F.R. **p. 148**
Bd, Sv	Gl	Often in much thicker vegetation than the next species, but will tolerate areas of shorter grass. **p. 148**
Lc	Gs	Has been recorded in Thyolo district in suitable habitat. **p. 148**
Vw	Gs	A pair recorded displaying in Vwaza Marsh G.R.; must now be unusual outside Kasungu and Nyika N.P. **p. 138**
Vw, Be	Gs, Dw	Becoming scarce outside protected areas. **p. 138**
Lc, Sr	Ma	**p. 104**
Cd	Gs	There are a few recent records from the south. **p. 102**
Bd, Sv	Dw	Has been seen at Kasinthula Fishponds. **p. 102**
Lc	Dw, Ma	No recent records. **p. 102**
Cd	Ma	Usually in thicker swamp than the African Crake. **p. 100**
Ll, Cd	Dw	Present in summer only. **p. 100**

BOM	Family / species	Stat.	Al.	Ra.	Nat. Park
130	Black Crake *Amaurornis flavirostris*	C/Re	ML	T	– K Li –
131	Buffspotted Flufftail *Sarothrura elegans*	U/Re	M	T	– – – –
132	Redchested Flufftail *S. rufa*	F/Re	HM	T	N – – –
132A	Longtoed Flufftail *S. lugens*	R/Re	M	C	– – – –
133	Streakybreasted Flufftail *S. boehmi*	USRe	ML	CS	– K – –
134	Striped Flufftail *S. affinis*	U/Re	H	NS	N – – –
135	Lesser Moorhen *Gallinula angulata*	USRe	ML	T	– – – –
136	Moorhen *G. chloropus*	C/Re	ML	T	– – Li –
137	Purple Gallinule *Porphyrio porphyrio*	F/Re	ML	T	– – Li –
138	Lesser Gallinule *Porphyrula alleni*	U/Re	ML	T	– – Li –
139	Redknobbed Coot *Fulica cristata*	C/Re	A	T	N K – –
140	**Finfoots** HELIORNITHIDAE African Finfoot *Podica senegalensis*	U/Re	ML	T	– – – –
141	**Bustards and korhaans** OTIDIDAE Stanley's Bustard *Neotis denhami*	ULRe	H	N	N – – –
142	Blackbellied Korhaan *Eupodotis melanogaster*	U/Re	ML	T	N K Li L
143	**Jacanas** JACANIDAE African Jacana *Actophilornis africanus*	V/Re	ML	T	– K Li –
144	Lesser Jacana *Microparra capensis*	F/Re	ML	CS	– K Li –
145	**Painted snipes** ROSTRATULIDAE Painted Snipe *Rostratula benghalensis*	U/Re	ML	CS	– K – L
146	**Plovers** CHARADRIIDAE Blacksmith Plover *Vanellus armatus*	F/Re	ML	T	– K Li –

Local.	Habitat	Comments
Em	Ma	Soon colonises even the smallest dams. **p. 102**
Ld, Mj	Th, Ef	Submontane evergreen forest; calls during the rains at dusk or at night. **p. 102**
Bd ,Cd	Dw	Like all flufftails more likely to be heard than seen. **p. 102**
Dz	Dw	Known from one record to date in the Dzalanyama F.R., inhabiting short grass at the edge of a dambo. **p. 100**
Cd	Dw	Usually in seasonally inundated grassland rather than permanent swamp. Present in summer only. **p. 100**
Vi, Mj	Bb, Gs	More common in montane grassland, where it calls at dusk and at night. **p. 100**
Be, Sr	Dw	Prefers temporary pools to permanent marsh. Present in summer only. **p. 98**
Mp, Em	Ma, Ow	Permanent marsh, unlikely alongside the last species. **p. 98**
Mp, Em	Ma	Usually in large areas of marsh where thick reeds occur. **p. 98**
Lc, Em	Ma	Likes smaller areas of water than the previous species, particularly dams fringed by reeds. **p. 98**
Lc, Em	Ma, Ow	**p. 96**
Ld, Sr	Ri	Inhabits both large and small rivers with shaded banks. **p. 84**
Vi	Gs	Confined to the Nyika and Viphya Plateaux. **p. 134**
Dz	Br, Gs	**p. 136**
Mp, Em	Ma	**p. 118**
Mp, Em	Ma	Much less common than the previous species. **p. 118**
Lm, Cd	Dw, Mf, Ri	**p. 104**
Mp, Em	Dw, Mf	**p. 122**

BOM	Family / species	Stat.	Al.	Ra.	Nat. Park
147	Lesser Blackwinged Plover *V. lugubris*	U/Re	ML	T	– K Li L
148	Crowned Plover *V. coronatus*	F/Re	ML	T	– – Li –
149	Longtoed Plover *V. crassirostris*	F/Re	ML	T	– – Li –
149A	Whitecrowned Plover *V. albiceps*	RLRe	L	S	– – – –
150	Wattled Plover *V. senegallus*	F/Re	ML	T	N K Li –
150A	American Golden Plover *Pluvialis dominica*	RSVi	L	C	– – – –
151	Grey Plover *P. squatarola*	USVi	ML	CS	– K – –
152	Ringed Plover *Charadrius hiaticula*	VSVi	ML	T	N K Li –
153	Threebanded Plover *C. tricollaris*	C/Re	ML	T	N K – L
154	Kittlitz's Plover *C. pecuarius*	V/Re	ML	T	– – – –
155	Whitefronted Plover *C. marginatus*	ULRe	ML	T	– – – –
156	Sand Plover *C. leschenaultii*	RSVi	ML	NS	– – – –
157	Caspian Plover *C. asiaticus*	USVi	ML	T	N – – –
	Sandpipers, snipes, etc. SCOLOPACIDAE				
158	Whimbrel *Numenius phaeopus*	USVi	L	T	– – Li –
159	Curlew *N. arquata*	RSVi	L	S	N K – –
159A	Blacktailed Godwit *Limosa limosa*	RSVi	L	S	– – – –
160	Bartailed Godwit *L. lapponica*	RSVi	L	CS	– – – –
161	Greenshank *Tringa nebularia*	VSVi	A	T	N K Li L
162	Marsh Sandpiper *T. stagnatilis*	CSVi	ML	T	N K Li L
163	Wood Sandpiper *T. glareola*	ASVi	A	T	N K Li L
164	Green Sandpiper *T. ochropus*	FSVi	ML	T	N K – L

Local.	Habitat	Comments
Vw, Lc	Gs	Also found in light woodland. **p. 120**
Mp, Ll	Gs	Usually in pairs. **p. 122**
Vw, Lc	Ma, Mf	Often on mudflats at the edge of marshland. **p. 122**
Sr	Mf	Only on sandbanks around Chikwawa on the Shire River. **p. 122**
Vw, Ll	Gd	Inhabits short dry grassland. **p. 122**
Mp	Ow, Mf	Known from one record at Mpatsanjoka Dambo, but could occur elsewhere in the Lake Malawi or Shire valley littoral. **p. 120**
Mp, Lc	Ow, Mf	There are a few records of this species, some from dams. **p. 120**
Mp, Em	Ow, Mf	Young birds of this palaearctic species migrate in immature plumage. **p. 106**
Mp, Em	Ow, Mf	**p. 106**
Mp, Em	Mf	Common on sandbars and mudflats. **p. 106**
Lm, Sr	Mf	Regularly seen on sandbanks and occasionally on mudflats in the lower reaches of the Shire River. **p. 108**
Ka, Bd	Mf	No recent records. **p. 106**
Vw, Lc	Gs	Sometimes occurs in large numbers. **p. 104**
Sr, Em	Ow, Mf	Occasionally at Kasinthula Fishponds. **p. 124**
Lm, Lc	Ow, Mf	There are two recent records from Lake Malombe and Lake Chilwa. **p. 124**
Mp	Mf	Known from one record at Mpatsanjoka Dambo. **p. 118**
Lm, Sr	Ow, Mf	Recorded on the Shire River near Chikwawa and at Lumbadzi sewage works at Lilongwe. **p. 118**
Mp, Em	Ma, Ow, Mf	**p. 108**
Mp, Em	Ma, Ow, Mf	**p. 108**
Mp, Em	Ma, Ow, Mf	**p. 112**
Ld, Em	Ma, Ow, Mf	Common at Limbe sewage works. **p. 118**

BOM	Family / species	Stat.	Al.	Ra.	Nat. Park
165	Common Sandpiper *T. hypoleucos*	ASVi	A	T	N K Li L
166	Spotted Redshank *T. erythropus*	RSVi	L	S	– – – –
167	Redshank *T. totanus*	RSVi	ML	CS	– – – –
168	Terek Sandpiper *Xenus cinereus*	USVi	ML	CS	– – – –
169	Turnstone *Arenaria interpres*	RSVi	L	CS	– – – –
170	Great Snipe *Gallingo media*	USVi	ML	T	N – – –
171	African Snipe *G. nigripennis*	U/Re	ML	T	N K – –
172	Common (European) Snipe *G. gallinago*	RSVi	M	N	– – – –
173	Curlew Sandpiper *Calidris ferruginea*	CSVi	ML	T	N – – –
174	Little Stint *C. minuta*	VSVi	ML	T	N K Li –
175	Sanderling *C. alba*	RSVi	ML	CS	N – – –
176	Broadbilled Sandpiper *Limicola falcinellus*	RSVi	H	N	N – – –
177	Ruff *Philomachus pugnax*	VSVi	ML	T	N K Li –
	Stilts and avocets RECURVIROSTRIDAE				
178	Blackwinged Stilt *Himantopus himantopus*	V/Re	ML	T	N K Li –
179	Avocet *Recurvirostra avosetta*	UWVi	ML	CS	– – Li –
	Dikkops BURHINIDAE				
180	Spotted Dikkop *Burhinus capensis*	F/Re	A	T	N K Li –
181	Water Dikkop *B. vermiculatus*	F/Re	ML	T	– K Li –
	Coursers and pratincoles GLAREOLIDAE				
182	Temminck's Courser *Cursorius temminckii*	F/Re	A	T	N K – –
182A	Threebanded Courser *Rhinoptilus cinctus*	R/Va	H	N	– – – –
183	Bronzewinged Courser *R. chalcopterus*	F/Re	ML	T	N K Li L

Local.	Habitat	Comments
	*	Any water habitat; a few overwinter. **p. 118**
Lm, Em	Ow, Mf	Several sight records at Kasinthula Fishponds. **p. 118**
Bd, Em	Ow, Mf	Also recorded at Kasinthula Fishponds. **p. 118**
Mp, Lc	Ma, Ow, Mf	Has been recorded at Bunda Dam, Liwonde sewage works and Kasinthula Fishponds. **p. 114**
Lm	Ow, Mf	Only one record to date from Lake Malawi, occurrence elsewhere possible in suitable habitat. **p. 114**
Be, Lc	Dw	Seasonally quite common at Lake Chilwa. **p. 104**
Be, Cd	Dw	**p. 104**
	Dw	*See page 2.*
Mp, Em	Ma, Ow, Mf	**p. 112**
Mp, Em	Ma, Ow, Mf	**p. 110**
Mp, Lc	Mf	Recent records from scattered localities throughout the country. **p. 114**
	Ow	No recent records. **p. 110**
Mp, Em	Ma, Ow, Mf	**p. 108**
Mp, Em	Ma, Ow, Mf	**p. 126**
Lm, Em	Ma, Ow	Has been seen at Kasinthula Fishponds. **p. 126**
Sv	Gs	Common on earth roads at night in Kasungu district. **p. 128**
Lm, Sr	Ow, Ri	This and the previous species are mainly nocturnal. **p. 128**
Be, Cd	Gs	Only in very short grass or on bare ground. **p. 130**
Vi	Gs	One accepted record from the Viphya Plateau. **p. 130**
Ll	Gs	Nocturnal, mostly on bare ground or earth roads. **p. 130**

BOM	Family / species	Stat.	Al.	Ra.	Nat. Park
184	Redwinged Pratincole *Glareola pratincola*	V/Re	ML	T	N K Li –
184A	Blackwinged pratincole *G. nordmanni*	R/Vi	L	S	– – – –
185	Rock Pratincole *G. nuchalis*	RLRe	L	NS	– – – –
186	**Gulls and terns** LARIDAE Greyheaded Gull *Larus cirrocephalus*	A/RE	ML	T	N K Li –
186A	Blackheaded Gull *L. ridibundus*	RSVi	L	S	– – – –
187	Lesser Blackbacked Gull *L. fuscus*	RSVi	ML	NS	– – – –
188	Gullbilled Tern *Gelochelidon nilotica*	RSVi	ML	S	– – Li –
188A	Common Tern *Sterna hirundo*	RSVi	ML	S	– – – –
189	Sooty Tern *S. fuscata*	RSVa	M	S	– – – –
190	Whiskered Tern *Chlidonias hybridus*	USRe	ML	S	– – – –
191	Whitewinged Tern *C. leucopterus*	VSVi	ML	T	N K Li –
192	**Skimmers** RYNCHOPIDAE African Skimmer *Rynchops flavirostris*	ULRe	ML	T	– K Li –
193	**Sandgrouse** PTEROCLIDIDAE Doublebanded Sandgrouse *Pterocles bicinctus*	RLRe	L	S	– – – –
194	**Pigeons and doves** COLUMBIDAE Rameron Pigeon *Columba arquatrix*	F/Re	H	T	N – – –
195	Delegorgue's Pigeon *C. delegorguei*	RLRe	M	S	– – – –
196	Pinkbreasted Turtle Dove *Streptopelia lugens*	ULRe	H	N	N – – –
197	Redeyed Dove *S. semitorquata*	V/Re	ML	T	N K Li L
198	Mourning Dove *S. decipiens*	C/Re	ML	T	– – Li L
199	Cape Turtle Dove *S. capicola*	A/Re	ML	T	N K Li L
200	Laughing Dove *S. senegalensis*	V/Re	ML	T	N K Li L

Local.	Habitat	Comments
	Gs, Ma, Mf	Large flocks seen at Mpatsanjoka Dambo and Elephant Marsh. **p. 128**
Em	Gs, Ma, Mf	One record to date from the lower Shire valley; could occur in other areas of suitable habitat. **p. 128**
Sr	Ri	Present September to December on the Shire River where there are sufficient exposed rocks, between Matope and Kapuchira. **p. 128**
	Ma, Ow	**p. 52**
Lm	Ow	A rare palaearctic migrant known from one Lake Malawi record; could occur elsewhere. **p. 52**
Lm	Ow	There are a few scattered records of this species mostly from Lake Malawi. **p. 54**
Lm, Lc	Ow, Ri	Several recent records from the Shire River in Liwonde N.P. **p. 56**
Lm, Sr	Ow	Only three records to date, one from Thyolo district after Chiperone conditions. **p. 58**
Mj	Ow	Known from one old record in Mulanje district. **p. 60**
Lc, Em	Ma, Ow	This species has bred at Lake Chilwa; it is normally only present in summer. **p. 60**
	Ma, Ow	Much more common than the Whiskered Tern. **p. 60**
Vw, Sr	Ma, Mf, Ri	Breeds on sandbanks in the lower Shire River, present in summer; a few remain until May. **p. 54**
Sv	Ac	Recent records from Ngabu in the lower Shire valley. **p. 194**
De, Mj	Ef	Inhabits the canopy of montane and sometimes submontane evergreen forest. **p. 200**
Tm	Ef	Confined to the canopy of the submontane evergreen forest of Thyolo Mountain. **p. 198**
Mi	Ef	*See page 2.*
	*	**p. 196**
Ll	Ac	Generally in low-lying dry areas, but is found higher around Rumpi. **p. 196**
	Br, Mo, Ac	**p. 196**
	Ac	**p. 196**

BOM	Family / species	Stat.	Al.	Ra.	Nat. Park			
201	Namaqua Dove *Oena capensis*	F/Re	ML	T	–	K	–	L
202	Tambourine Dove *Turtur tympanistria*	C/Re	ML	T	N	–	Li	L
203	Bluespotted Dove *T. afer*	V/Re	M	T	N	K	Li	L
204	Emeraldspotted Dove *T. chalcospilos*	A/Re	ML	T	N	K	Li	L
205	Cinnamon Dove *Aplopelia larvata*	F/Re	HM	T	N	–	–	–
206	Green Pigeon *Treron calva*	C/Re	ML	T	N	K	Li	L
	Parrots and lovebirds PSITTACIDAE							
207	Cape Parrot *Poicephalus robustus suahelicus*	F/Re	A	T	N	K	Li	L
208	Brownheaded Parrot *P. cryptoxanthus*	F/Re	ML	CS	–	–	Li	L
209	Meyer's Parrot *P. meyeri*	F/Re	ML	NC	N	K	–	–
210	Lilian's Lovebird *Agapornis lilianae*	FLRe	L	S	–	–	Li	–
	Louries MUSOPHAGIDAE							
211	Livingstone's Lourie *Tauraco livingstoni*	C/Re	HM	S	–	–	–	–
211A	Schalow's Lourie *T. schalowi*	C/Re	HM	NC	N	K	–	–
212	Purplecrested Lourie *T. porphyreolophus*	C/Re	ML	T	N	K	Li	L
213	Grey Lourie *Corythaixoides concolor*	C/Re	ML	T	N	K	Li	L
214	Blackfaced Lourie *C. personata*	ULRe	M	N	–	–	–	–
	Cuckoos and coucals CUCULIDAE							
215	Great Spotted Cuckoo *Clamator glandarius*	FSRe	ML	T	N	–	–	–
216	Jacobin Cuckoo *C. jacobinus*	FSRe	A	T	N	K	–	L
217	Striped Cuckoo *C. levaillantii*	FSRe	ML	T	N	K	Li	L
218	Redchested Cuckoo *Cuculus solitarius*	CSRe	A	T	N	K	–	L
219	Black Cuckoo *C. clamosus*	FSRe	ML	T	N	K	Li	L

Local.	Habitat	Comments
Lc, Sv	Br, Ac	Fairly common where soils are sandy. **p. 196**
	Th, Ef	Common in the ground stratum of riparian and submontane evergreen forest. **p. 198**
Dz, Bd	Br, Ac	Rarely alongside the next species. **p. 200**
	Ac, Mo	Usually at lower altitudes than the Bluespotted Dove. **p. 200**
Vi, Tm	Ef	Inhabits the ground stratum of montane and submontane evergreen forest. **p. 198**
	Br, Ac	Flocks often gather at fruiting trees. **p. 198**
Ph, Bd	Br, Ac	This is the east African race. Generally in richer woodland than the Brownheaded Parrot. **p. 202**
Sv, Lm	Br, Mo, Ac	**p. 202**
Ch, Ld	Br, Ac	Common in Lilongwe district. **p. 202**
	Mo, Ac	Apparently now confined to Liwonde N.P., where common. **p. 204**
Tm, Mj	Ef	East of the Rift more or less confined to evergreen forest. **p. 206**
Ld, Ns	Ef, Br	*See page 4.*
	Br	Rarely occurs alongside the Schalow's Lourie. **p. 206**
	Ac	This species and the Blackfaced Lourie have mutually exclusive distributions. **p. 206**
Ch	Br, Ac	*See page 4.*
De, Sv	*	The next six cuckoo species, all African migrants, are found in Malawi only during the summer months. **p. 212**
	Br, Ac	**p. 208**
Ld, Sv	Br, Ac	Common in the central region. **p. 208**
	*	Occurs in any woodland habitat in addition to all types of evergreen forest. **p. 210**
Ld, Za	Br, Ac	**p. 212**

BOM	Family / species	Stat.	Al.	Ra.	Nat. Park
220	African Cuckoo *C. gularis*	CSRe	A	T	N K Li L
220A	European Cuckoo *C. canorus*	FSVi	A	T	N K – –
221	Lesser Cuckoo *C. poliocephalus*	RWVi	M	S	– – – –
221A	Madagascar Lesser Cuckoo *C. rochii*	USVi	L	S	– – – –
222	Thickbilled Cuckoo *Pachycoccyx audeberti*	U/Re	ML	NS	– – – L
223	Barred Cuckoo *Cercococcyx montanus*	R/Re	L	S	– – – L
224	Klaas's Cuckoo *Chrysococcyx klaas*	V/Re	A	T	N K Li L
225	Diederik Cuckoo *C. caprius*	CSRe	ML	T	N K Li L
226	Emerald Cuckoo *C. cupreus*	F/Re	ML	T	N – Li L
227	Green Coucal *Ceuthmochares aereus*	F/Re	ML	T	– – Li L
228	Black Coucal *Centropus bengalensis*	U/Re	ML	T	– K Li –
229	Copperytailed Coucal *C. cupreicaudus*	ULRe	M	C	– – – –
230	Senegal Coucal *C. senegalensis*	U/Re	M	T	N K – –
231	Whitebrowed Coucal *C. superciliosus*	C/Re	A	N	N – – –
231A	Burchell's Coucal *C. burchellii*	V/Re	ML	CS	– K Li L
Barn Owls TYTONIDAE					
232	Barn owl *Tyto alba*	F/Re	ML	T	– K – L
233	Grass Owl *T. capensis*	U/Re	HM	T	N – – –
Owls STRIGIDAE					
234	Scops Owl *Otus senegalensis*	F/Re	ML	T	N K Li –
235	Whitefaced Owl *O. leucotis*	U/Re	ML	T	– K – L
236	Cape Eagle Owl *Bubo capensis*	RLRe	HL	T	– – – –

Local.	Habitat	Comments
	*	Very difficult to distinguish from the European Cuckoo, but has more yellow at the base of the bill. **p. 210**
Ld, Bd	*	Presumably occurs in all Malawi's national parks. **p. 210**
De, Sv	*	Very similar to the Madagascar Lesser Cuckoo, but is present only in summer from November to April. **p. 210**
Sv	Th	Not illustrated in the text as its plumage is almost the same as that of the previous species; present April to September.
Ll, Sv	Br, Mo	Recorded from sparse Brachystegia woodland on the eastern side of Lake Malawi. **p. 212**
Sv	Th, Ef	Has been seen flying over sugarcane fields at Sucoma. **p. 210**
	*	Prefers richer woodland than the next species. **p. 208**
	*	Usually only in drier areas, present in summer only. **p. 208**
Ld, Bd	Th, Ef	Calls from the canopy of riparian evergreen forest. **p. 208**
Sv	Th, Ef	Fairly common in thicket, also in riparian and submontane evergreen forest, always in the canopy. **p. 212**
Lc, Cd,	Gl, Ma	**p. 212**
	Ma	Upper reaches of the Bua River in Papyrus reedbeds. **p. 214**
	Gl	Very sparse; has been recorded in Rumpi district. **p. 214**
Ch, Ka	*	Found from the latitude of the Viphya Plateau northwards. **p. 214**
	*	Occurs south of the Viphya Plateau. **p. 214**
Bd	Br, Ro	Must now be dependent on buildings. **p. 216**
De, Mj	Bb, Gm	Difficult to tell from the Barn Owl, but has a darker back. **p. 216**
Ld, Ll	Br, Ac	Common in Lilongwe district. **p. 218**
	Br, Ac	Has been seen in Thyolo district. **p. 218**
Mj	Ro	The only recent records are from Mulanje Mountain and Mwabvi Game Reserve. **p. 220**

BOM	Family / species	Stat.	Al.	Ra.	Nat. Park
237	Spotted Eagle owl *B. africanus*	C/Re	A	T	N K Li L
238	Giant Eagle Owl *B. lacteus*	F/Re	ML	T	N K Li L
239	Pel's Fishing Owl *Scotopelia peli*	ULRe	ML	T	– – Li L
240	Pearlspotted Owl *Glaucidium perlatum*	F/Re	ML	T	– K – –
241	Barred Owl *G. capense*	F/Re	ML	T	– – Li L
242	Wood Owl *Strix woodfordii*	C/Re	A	T	N – Li L
243	Marsh Owl *Asio capensis*	U/Re	A	T	N K – –
244	**Nightjars** CAPRIMULGIDAE European Nightjar *Caprimulgus europaeus*	FSVi	ML	T	N – Li L
245	Fierynecked Nightjar *C. pectoralis*	V/Re	ML	T	N K Li L
246	Mountain Nightjar *C. poliocephalus*	F/Re	H	N	N – – –
247	Freckled Nightjar *C. tristigma*	F/Re	A	T	N K ––
248	Mozambique Nightjar *C. fossii*	V/Re	ML	T	– K Li L
249	Pennantwinged Nightjar *Macrodipteryx vexillaria*	CSRe	ML	T	N K Li –
250	**Swifts and spinetails** APODIDAE Scarce Swift *Schoutedenapus myoptilus*	ULVi	H	T	N – – –
251	Mottled Spinetail *Telecanthura ussheri*	U/Re	L	S	– – – L
252	Böhm's Spinetail *Neafrapus boehmi*	U/Re	L	S	– – – L
253	Palm Swift *Cypsiurus parvus*	V/Re	ML	T	N K Li L
254	Alpine Swift *Apus melba*	U/Re	HM	NS	N – – –
255	Mottled Swift *A. aequatorialis*	F/Re	HM	T	N – – –
256	Black Swift *A. barbatus*	V/Re	A	T	N K – –
257	Eurasian Swift *A. apus*	ASVi	A	T	N K Li L

Local.	Habitat	Comments
	Br, Mo, Ac	Hunts on earth roads at night. **p. 220**
Sv	*	Breeds in riparian evergreen forest. **p. 220**
Lm, Sr	Ow, Ri	Requires large trees in palm or deciduous thickets, near water. **p. 222**
Ld, Ll	Br, Mo, Ac	**p. 218**
	Th, Ef	**p. 218**
	Br, Th, Ef	Occurs in all types of evergreen forest. **p. 216**
Cd, Sr	Ma	As its name infers, only regular in marshes. **p. 216**
Bd	Br, Ac	Quite common in Thyolo district. Summer only. **p 224**
	Br, Ac	Feeds from earth roads at night. **p. 224**
Mi, Vi	Ef, Gs	***See page 4.***
Dz, Ph	Br, Ro	Favours rock slabs in Brachystegia woodland. **p. 224**
	Br, Mo, Ac	Very common at low altitudes, feeding from earth roads. **p. 224**
Bd	Br, Ac	Common on earth roads at night, present in summer. **p. 224**
Mi, Mj	*	Fairly common on the Nyika Plateau and Mulanje Mountain. **p 242**
Sv	Ac	Usually near water where there are baobabs. **p. 242**
Sv	Ac	Only in the lower Shire valley; has been recorded in Mwabvi Game Reserve. **p. 242**
	*	Breeds and roosts in any type of palm. **p. 240**
Mi, Mj	Ro	This and all subsequent swift species are strong fliers and can be found far from their preferred habitat. **p. 240**
De, Mj	Ro	Wanders to lower altitudes in inclement weather. **p. 242**
De, Mj	Ro	Difficult to tell from the next species but likely to be seen in small groups. **p. 240**
	*	Usually in large numbers, often congregating at termite hatches. Summer only. **p. 242**

BOM	Family / species	Stat.	Al.	Ra.	Nat. Park
258	Little Swift *A. affinis*	F/Re	ML	T	N – – –
259	Horus Swift *A. horus*	U/Re	L	CS	– – – L
260	Whiterumped Swift *A. caffer*	F/Re	A	T	N K Li –
261	**Mousebirds** COLIIDAE Speckled Mousebird *Colius striatus*	F/Re	A	T	N – – L
262	Redfaced Mousebird *C. indicus*	C/Re	ML	CS	– – Li L
263	**Trogons** TROGONIDAE Narina Trogon *Apaloderma narina*	F/Re	ML	T	N – Li L
264	Bartailed Trogon *A. vittatum*	F/Re	HM	T	N – – –
265	**Kingfishers** HALCYONIDAE Giant Kingfisher *Ceryle maxima*	F/Re	A	T	N K Li –
266	Pied Kingfisher *C. rudis*	V/Re	ML	T	N K Li L
267	Halfcollared Kingfisher *Alcedo semitorquata*	ULRe	ML	T	N – Li –
268	Malachite Kingfisher *A. cristata*	V/Re	ML	T	N K Li L
269	Pygmy Kingfisher *Ispidina picta*	FSRe	ML	T	N K – L
270	Woodland Kingfisher *Halcyon senegalensis*	FSRe	ML	T	N K Li L
271	Striped Kingfisher *H. chelicuti*	V/Re	ML	T	– K Li L
272	Brownhooded Kingfisher *H. albiventris*	C/Re	ML	T	N K Li L
273	Greyhooded Kingfisher *H. leucocephala*	FSRe	ML	T	N K Li L
274	**Bee-eaters** MEROPIDAE European Bee-eater *Merops apiaster*	ASVi	A	T	N K Li L
275	Bluecheeked Bee-eater *M. persicus*	FSVi	ML	T	N K Li L
275A	Olive Bee-eater *M. superciliosus*	FSVi	ML	T	N K Li L

Local.	Habitat	Comments
Ld, Sv	Ro	Utilises man-made structures, particularly bridges. **p. 240**
Sv	*	May be seen at Chikwawa nesting in holes recently vacated by Carmine Bee-eaters. **p. 240**
Ld, Sv	*	**p. 240**
De, Sv	Bb, Gl	**p. 244**
	Ac, Gl	**p. 244**
Mj	Th, Ef	Common in riparian evergreen forest, occasionally thicket. **p. 204**
Vi, Mj	Ef	*See page 4.*
Sr	Ow, Ri	**p. 248**
	*	Any water habitat. **p. 248**
Za, Mj	Ri	Normally only near small, heavily wooded streams. **p. 252**
	*	Any water habitat. **p. 252**
Mj	*	Inhabits any woodland or evergreen forest, present only in summer; some individuals remain into early winter. **p. 252**
Sv	Ac	Usually in dry woodland away from water, present in summer only. **p. 250**
	Br, Mo, Ac	Any woodland away from water. **p. 252**
	*	Found in any type of woodland, usually near water. **p. 252**
Ld, Ll	Br, Mo, Ac	Not normally near water, present only in summer. **p. 250**
	*	**p. 246**
Mp, Em	*	Usually near water, but all bee-eaters are strong fliers and wander away from the habitat they prefer. **p. 246**
Mp, Dz	*	Normally away from water. **p. 246**

BOM	Family / species	Stat.	Al.	Ra.	Nat. Park
276	Carmine Bee-eater *M. nubicoides*	FSRe	ML	T	N K Li L
277	Böhm's Bee-eater *M. boehmi*	FLRe	L	CS	– – Li L
278	Little Bee-eater *M. pusillus*	V/Re	ML	T	N K Li L
279	Whitefronted Bee-eater *M. bullockoides*	U/Re	ML	T	N K Li –
280	Swallowtailed Bee-eater *M. hirundineus*	U/Re	ML	T	N K Li L
	Rollers CORACIIDAE				
281	European Roller *Coracias garrulus*	FSVi	ML	T	N K Li L
282	Lilacbreasted Roller *C. caudata*	V/Re	ML	T	N K Li L
283	Racket-tailed Roller *C. spatulata*	U/Re	ML	T	– K Li L
284	Purple Roller *C. naevia*	R/Re	ML	CS	– – – L
285	Broadbilled Roller *Eurystomus glaucurus*	VSRe	ML	T	N K Li L
	Hoopoes UPUPIDAE				
286	Hoopoe *Upupa epops*	C/Re	ML	T	N K Li L
	Woodhoopoes PHOENICULIDAE				
287	Redbilled Woodhoopoe *Phoeniculus purpureus*	F/Re	ML	T	N K Li L
288	Scimitarbilled Woodhoopoe *P. cyanomelas*	F/Re	ML	T	N K Li L
	Hornbills BUCEROTIDAE				
289	Grey Hornbill *Tockus nasutus*	V/Re	ML	T	N K Li L
290	Redbilled Hornbill *T. erythrorhynchus*	V/Re	ML	T	– – Li L
291	Yellowbilled Hornbill *T. flavirostris*	U/Re	L	S	– – – L
292	Palebilled Hornbill *T. pallidirostris*	U/Re	ML	T	N K Li –
293	Crowned Hornbill *T. alboterminatus*	V/Re	A	T	N K Li L
294	Trumpeter Hornbill *Bycanistes bucinator*	C/Re	A	T	N K Li L

Local.	Habitat	Comments
Sr	Ri	This species nests in the sand cliffs of large rivers; there is a large colony on the Shire River at Chikwawa. **p. 246**
Sv	Th	Inhabits thicket near water where there is cover. **p. 244**
	*	**p. 246**
Sr	Ri	In similar habitat to Carmine Bee-eaters. **p. 246**
Ll, Sv	Br, Ac	Not regular in any particular area, may be an African migrant. **p. 244**
Ll, Bd	Br, Mo, Ac	**p. 254**
	Br, Ac	Very common at low levels, preferring light woodland. **p. 254**
Ph	Br, Mo	Confined to the drier areas of Brachystegia and Mopane woodland. **p. 254**
Vw	Ac	Individuals have been seen recently at Vwaza Marsh, Nkhata Bay and in the lower Shire valley. **p. 254**
	Br, Ac	Two races occur and both are present in summer. The Madagascar form does not breed in Malawi. **p. 254**
	Br, Mo, Ac	There are two races in Malawi, one resident and the other a palaearctic migrant. **p. 256**
Dz, Ph	Br, Mo, Ac	Sometimes alongside the next species. **p. 256**
Dz, Ph	Br, Mo, Ac	**p. 256**
	Br, Mo, Ac	**p. 258**
	Mo, Ac	Commonest at low altitudes. **p. 258**
Sv	Ac	Confined to the lower Shire valley. **p. 258**
Za, Bd	Br	*See page 4.*
	*	Generally in riparian or submontane evergreen forest as well as other woodland habitats. **p. 258**
	*	In any relatively rich woodland, including evergreen forest. **p. 260**

BOM	Family / species	Stat.	Al.	Ra.	Nat. Park			
295	Silverycheeked Hornbill *B. brevis*	F/Re	HM	T	N	–	–	–
296	Ground Hornbill *Bucorvus leadbeateri*	F/Re	ML	T	N	K	Li	L
	Barbets CAPITONIDAE							
297	Brownbreasted Barbet *Lybius melanopterus*	ULRe	L	NS	–	–	Li	–
298	Blackbacked Barbet *L. minor*	ULRe	M	N	N	–	–	–
299	Blackcollared Barbet *L. torquatus*	V/Re	ML	T	N	K	Li	L
300	Miombo Pied Barbet *L. frontatus*	F/Re	M	NC	N	K	–	–
301	White-eared Barbet *Stactolaema leucotis*	F/Re	M	S	–	–	–	–
302	Green Barbet *Buccanodon olivaceum*	CLRe	HM	NS	–	–	–	–
303	Whyte's Barbet *Stactolaema whytii*	F/Re	M	T	–	K	–	–
304	Moustached Green Tinkerbird *Pogoniulus leucomystax*	C/Re	HM	T	N	–	–	–
305	Green Tinker Barbet *P. simplex*	ULRe	M	S	–	–	–	–
306	Yellowfronted Tinker Barbet *P. chrysoconus*	V/Re	ML	T	N	K	Li	L
307	Goldenrumped Tinker Barbet *P. bilineatus*	V/Re	ML	NS	N	–	Li	L
308	Crested Barbet *Trachyphonus vaillantii*	U/Re	ML	T	–	K	Li	L
	Honeyguides INDICATORIDAE							
309	Scalythroated Honeyguide *Indicator variegatus*	F/Re	ML	T	N	K	–	–
310	Greater Honeyguide *I. indicator*	F/Re	ML	T	N	K	Li	L
311	Lesser Honeyguide *I. minor*	F/Re	ML	T	N	K	–	L
312	Eastern Honeyguide *I. meliphilus*	U/Re	M	NS	N	–	–	–
313	Slenderbilled Honeyguide *Prodotiscus zambesiae*	U/Re	ML	CS	N	K	–	–
314	Sharpbilled Honeyguide *P. regulus*	U/Re	ML	CS	–	–	Li	–

Local.	Habitat	Comments
Mi, Mj	Ef	Any evergreen forest, except lowland. In the north occurs at high altitudes. **p. 260**
Sv, Ll	Br, Mo, Ac	**p. 262**
	Mo, Ac	*See page 6.*
Ch	Ef	*See page 6.*
	Br, Ac	The rare form with a yellowish face has been seen at Lake Chilwa. **p. 264**
Ch, Dz	Br	*See page 6.*
Za, Mj	Ef	Canopy of riparian or submontane evergreen forest. **p. 262**
Mi, Tm	Ef	*See page 6.*
Dz, Bd	Br	More common in the central region than elsewhere. **p. 262**
Mi, Mj	Ef	*See page 6.*
	Ef	East of the Rift from Mangochi Mountain northwards in the canopy of riparian and submontane evergreen forest. **p. 264**
	Br, Ac	**p. 266**
	Th, Ef	Calls in the canopy of riparian and submontane evergreen forest. **p. 264**
Bd	Mo, Ac	**p. 264**
Tm, Mj	*	Occurs in any evergreen forest. **p. 272**
Sv	Br, Mo, Ac	**p. 272**
Ld, Sv	*	Often in thickets or riparian evergreen forest. **p. 272**
Tm, Mj	Br, Ef	Riparian or submontane evergreen forest. **p. 274**
Dz, Ph	Br	**p. 274**
Ld, Bd	Br, Ac	**p. 272**

BOM	Family / species	Stat.	Al.	Ra.	Nat. Park
	Woodpeckers PICIDAE				
316	Bennett's Woodpecker *Campethera bennettii*	F/Re	ML	T	N K Li L
317	Goldentailed Woodpecker *C. abingoni*	F/Re	ML	T	N K Li L
318	Little Spotted Woodpecker *C. cailliautii*	U/Re	ML	T	N K – L
319	Cardinal Woodpecker *Dendropicos fuscescens*	V/Re	ML	T	N K Li L
320	Stierling's Woodpecker *D. stierlingi*	U/Re	M	CS	– – – –
321	Olive Woodpecker *Mesopicos griseocephalus*	F/Re	H	N	N – – –
322	Bearded Woodpecker *Thripias namaquus*	F/Re	ML	T	N K Li L
	Broadbills EURYLAIMIDAE				
323	African Broadbill *Smithornis capensis*	F/Re	A	T	N – – L
	Pittas PITTIDAE				
324	African Pitta *Pitta angolensis*	RSRe	M	T	N – – –
	Larks ALAUDIDAE				
325	Rufousnaped Lark *Mirafra africana*	FLRe	HM	NS	N – – –
326	Flappet Lark *M. rufocinnamomea*	C/Re	ML	T	N K Li L
327	Dusky Lark *Pinarocorys nigricans*	RWVi	M	CS	– – – –
328	Redcapped Lark *Calandrella cinerea*	C/Re	ML	T	N K Li –
329	Chestnutbacked Finchlark *Eremopterix leucotis*	C/Re	ML	T	– K – L
330	Fischer's Finchlark *E. leucopareia*	ULRe	M	N	– – – –
	Martins and swallows HIRUNDINIDAE				
331	Banded Martin *Riparia cincta*	F/Re	A	T	N – Li –
332	European Sand Martin *R. riparia*	FSVi	A	T	N K – L
333	Brownthroated Martin *R. paludicola*	F/Re	ML	T	N K Li –
334	European Swallow *Hirundo rustica*	ASVi	A	T	N K Li L

Local.	Habitat	Comments
Dz, Ph	Br, Ac	Two races occur, generally *C.b. scriptoricauda* east and *C. b. bennettii* west of the Rift, but there is some overlap. **p. 268**
Tm, Mj	*	Any woodland habitat including riparian and submontane evergreen forest. **p. 268**
Dz	Br, Th, Ef	Usually in Brachystegia woodland, occasionally thicket or edges of riparian evergreen forest. **p. 270**
	*	**p. 268**
Dz, Ph	Br	*See page 6.*
Mi, Vi	Ef	Inhabits the canopy and mid-stratum of montane evergreen forest. **p. 266**
Dz, Ph	Br, Ac	**p. 268**
Nk, Tm	Th, Ef	Mid-stratum of riparian and submontane evergreen forest. **p. 274**
Mp, Mj	Th, Ef	Found in thicket and riparian evergreen forest; probably only present in summer. **p. 274**
	Gs	Outside the Nyika N.P. only found west of the Rift in the Mangochi and Namizimu F.R. **p. 280**
	Br, Ac, Gs	**p. 278**
Ka	Gs	There are very few recent records of this species; one is from near Dowa. **p. 280**
	Gs	Populations fluctuate seasonally; it is least common during the rains. **p. 280**
	Gs	**p. 286**
	Gs	*See page 10.*
Mp, Ld	Gs, Ma	**p. 236**
Lc, Em	*	Usually near water, but on passage in other habitats. **p. 234**
Lc, Sr	Ow, Ri	Rarely far from water. **p. 236**
	*	**p. 232**

BOM	Family / species	Stat.	Al.	Ra.	Nat. Park
335	Angola Swallow *H. angolensis*	RLRe	H	N	N – – –
336	Blue Swallow *H. atrocaerulea*	USRe	H	T	N – – –
337	Wiretailed Swallow *H. smithii*	V/Re	ML	T	N K Li L
338	Whitethroated Swallow *H. albigularis*	U/Re	HL	T	N – – L
339	Pearlbreasted Swallow *H. dimidiata*	F/Re	M	T	– K – –
340	Redbreasted Swallow *H. semirufa*	U/Re	M	T	– K – –
341	Mosque Swallow *H. senegalensis*	F/Re	ML	T	N K Li L
342	Redrumped Swallow *H. daurica*	U/Re	HM	T	N K – –
343	Greater Striped Swallow *H. cucullata*	RSVi	HL	NS	N – – –
344	Lesser Striped Swallow *H. abyssinica*	V/Re	ML	T	N K Li L
345	Greyrumped Swallow *Pseudhirundo griseopyga*	C/Re	A	T	N K Li L
345A	South African Cliff Swallow *Hirundo spilodera*	R/Va	M	S	– – – –
346	Rock Martin *H. fuligula*	F/Re	A	T	N K Li L
347	House Martin *Delichon urbica*	VSVi	A	T	N K Li L
348	Eastern Saw-wing Swallow *Psalidoprocne orientalis*	C/Re	A	T	N – Li L
348A	Black Saw-wing Swallow *P. holomelas*	R/Re	L	S	– – – –
349	Whiteheaded Saw-wing Swallow *P. albiceps*	FSRe	HM	N	N – – –
350	Mascarene Martin *Phedina borbonica*	RSVi	ML	S	– – – –
351	**Drongos** DICRURIDAE Squaretailed Drongo *Dicrurus ludwigii*	C/Re	ML	S	– – – L
352	Forktailed Drongo *D. adsimilis*	V/Re	ML	T	N K Li L
353	**Orioles** ORIOLIDAE European Golden Oriole *Oriolus oriolus*	USVi	ML	T	N K Li L

Local.	Habitat	Comments
Mi	Gs	Only in small numbers on the Nyika Plateau and Misuku Hills. **p. 230**
Za, Mj	Gs	Fairly common over montane grassland on the Nyika and Mulanje Plateaux; present in summer only. **p. 230**
	*	Nests in any building. **p. 232**
Mj, Sv	Gs	Normally at high altitudes, but has been seen in low-lying areas in small numbers. **p. 230**
Ld, Dz	Br	Only in clearings in Brachystegia woodland, more common in central and northern areas. **p. 232**
Ld, De	Gs, Dw	Found in open grassland and cultivated areas in the Brachystegia belt. **p. 228**
Ld, Za	*	More associated with wooded rocky hills than the previous species. **p. 228**
De, Mj	*	*See page 8.*
Sv	*	To date only recorded on passage in the lower Shire valley. **p. 228**
	*	**p. 228**
	Gs, Dw	**p. 232**
Bd	*	There is one accepted record from the Blantyre district. **p. 230**
De, Mj	Ro	Common near rocky hills and mountains. **p. 236**
	*	**p. 236**
	*	Often in the vicinity of submontane and riparian evergreen forest. **p. 234**
Sv	*	Only recorded in the lower Shire valley. **p. 234**
Mi, Vi	Br	*See page 8.*
Lc, Em	Ma, Ow	Most likely to be seen at Lake Chilwa. **p. 234**
Tm, Mj	Th, Ef	Only east of the Rift. Common in riparian and submontane evergreen forest and in thickets at Lengwe N.P. **p. 296**
	Br, Mo, Ac	**p. 296**
Tm, Mj	*	Occasionally in evergreen forest. Summer only. **p. 302**

BOM	Family / species	Stat.	Al.	Ra.	Nat. Park
354	African Golden Oriole *O. auratus*	C/Re	ML	T	N K Li L
355	Blackheaded Oriole *O. larvatus*	C/Re	ML	T	N K Li L
356	Greenheaded Oriole *O. chlorocephalus*	ULRe	M	S	– – – –
	Crows CORVIDAE				
357	Pied Crow *Corvus albus*	A/Re	A	T	N K Li L
358	Whitenecked Raven *C. albicollis*	C/Re	HM	T	N K Li –
	Tits PARIDAE				
359	Northern Grey Tit *Parus griseiventris*	F/Re	M	T	N K – –
360	Southern Black Tit *P. niger*	C/Re	ML	CS	– K Li L
361	Carp's Black Tit *P. carpi*	F/Re	HM	NC	N K – –
362	Rufousbellied Tit *P. rufiventris*	F/Re	M	T	N K – –
	Penduline tits REMIZIDAE				
363	Grey Penduline Tit *Anthoscopus caroli*	F/Re	ML	T	N K Li L
	Creepers SALPORNITHIDAE				
364	Spotted Creeper *Salpornis spilonotus*	U/Re	M	T	N K – –
	Babblers TIMALIIDAE				
365	Mountain Babbler *Alcippe abyssinica*	ULRe	HM	NS	N – – –
366	Mountain Illadopsis *Malacocinchla pyrrhoptera*	RLRe	H	N	N – – –
367	Arrowmarked Babbler *Turdoides jardineii*	C/Re	ML	T	N K Li L
	Cuckooshrikes CAMPEPHAGIDAE				
368	Whitebreasted Cuckooshrike *Coracina pectoralis*	C/Re	ML	T	N K Li L
369	Grey Cuckooshrike *C. caesia*	ULRe	M	S	– – – –
370	Black Cuckooshrike *Campephaga flava*	C/Re	M	T	N K Li L

Local.	Habitat	Comments
	*	Any woodland including evergreen forest. **p. 302**
	*	Occurs in the same habitat as the previous species. **p. 302**
Tm	Ef	Only east of the Rift in a few scattered submontane evergreen forests. Fairly common on Thyolo Mountain. **p. 300**
	*	**p. 300**
	Ro	Wanders in other habitats, adopting human settlements alongside the Pied Crow. **p. 300**
Dz, Ph	Br	Only found west of the Rift, in mixed bird parties within Brachystegia woodland. **p. 308**
	Mo, Ac, Th	Does not overlap with the next species except in the Kasungu district. **p. 308**
Ch, Vi	Br, Ac, Gs	**p. 308**
Dz, Ph	Br	**p. 308**
Dz, Ph	Br	**p. 344**
Dz, Ph	Br	Sometimes in mixed Brachystegia bird parties. **p. 274**
	Ef	*See page 8.*
	Ef	*See page 8.*
	*	Typically found in neglected cultivation, long rank grass or edge of thicket. **p. 310**
	Br, Mo, Ac	**p. 298**
Tm	Ef	Confined to the mid-stratum of the Thyolo Mountain submontane evergreen forest. **p. 298**
	Br, Th, Ef	Occurs in any woodland including riparian and submontane evergreen forest. **p. 298**

BOM	Family / species	Stat.	Al.	Ra.	Nat. Park
	Bulbuls PYCNONOTIDAE				
371	Blackeyed Bulbul *Pycnonotus barbatus*	A/Re	A	T	N K Li L
372	Sombre Bulbul *Andropadus importunus*	C/Re	L	T	– – Li L
373	Little Green Bulbul *A. virens*	F/Re	M	T	N – – –
374	Olivebreasted Mountain Bulbul *A. tephrolaemus*	C/Re	H	NS	N – – –
375	Stripecheeked Bulbul *A. milanjensis*	F/Re	HM	T	N – – –
376	Montane Bulbul *A. montanus*	FLRe	HM	N	– – – –
377	Yellowbellied Bulbul *Chlorocichla flaviventris*	C/Re	ML	T	– – Li L
378	Terrestrial Bulbul *Phyllastrepus terrestris*	C/Re	ML	T	– – Li L
379	Grey-olive Bulbul *P. cerviniventris*	F/Re	M	T	N – – –
380	Placid Bulbul *P. placidus*	F/Re	HM	T	– – – –
381	Yellowstreaked Bulbul *P. flavostriatus*	F/Re	HM	T	N – – –
382	Yellowspottted Nicator *Nicator gularis*	F/Re	ML	T	– – Li L
	Chats, robins, thrushes, etc. TURDIDAE				
383	Whinchat *Saxicola rubetra*	RSVi	HM	N	N K – –
384	Stonechat *S. torquata*	C/Re	HM	T	N K Li –
385	European Wheatear *Oenanthe oenanthe*	USVi	A	T	N – – –
386	Capped Wheatear *O. pileata*	FSRe	ML	T	L K – –
387	Familiar Chat *Cercomela familiaris*	C/Re	ML	T	N K Li –
388	Arnot's Chat *Thamnolaea arnoti*	F/Re	M	T	N K Li L
389	Mocking Chat *T. cinnamomeiventris*	F/Re	A	T	N K – –
390	Miombo Rock Thrush *Monticola angolensis*	F/Re	M	T	N K – –
390A	Boulder Chat *Pinarornis plumosus*	RLRe	M	CS	– – – –

Local.	Habitat	Comments
	*	**p. 306**
	Th	*See page 12.*
Mi, Tm	Ef	*See page 12.*
Za, Mj	Ef	*See page 12.*
Mi, Mj	Ef	Inhabits the mid-stratum of montane and submontane evergreen forest. **p. 306**
Mi	Ef	*See page 12.*
Ll	Th	Very similar to the Sombre Bulbul; both species occur together in the same habitat. **p. 304**
Ka	Th, Ef	Occasionally in riparian evergreen forest. **p. 304**
Nk, Tm	Ef	*See page 12.*
Mi, Tm	Ef	*See page 12.*
Tm, Mj	Ef	Inhabits the mid-stratum of montane and submontane evergreen forest. **p. 306**
Nk, Sv	Th, Ef	Usually in thicket but inhabits riparian evergreen forest at higher altitudes. **p. 304**
Vi	Gs	The preferred habitat of this species is grassland and open country. **p. 322**
	Bb, Gl	The only chat found in thick rank growth. **p. 324**
Vi, Cd	Gs	Prefers very short grass or bare ground. Summer only. **p. 318**
Mp, Lc	Gs	Habitat as for European Wheatear but much more common, present only in summer. **p. 318**
Dz, Ph	Br	Feeds on the ground, flies to the mid-stratum when disturbed. **p. 320**
Dz, Ph	Br, Mo	Forages in the ground stratum and low on tree trunks. **p. 318**
Dz, Ph	Ro	Around rock slabs in any wooded hills. **p. 316**
Dz, Ph	Br	Usually where there are rocks in Brachystegia woodland. **p. 314**
Dz	Ro	Can be found, very sparsely, on rocky outcrops in Brachystegia woodland between Mchinji and Neno. **p. 316**

BOM	Family / species	Stat.	Al.	Ra.	Nat. Park
390B	Rufous Bushchat *Erythropygia galactotes*	RSVi	L	S	– – – –
391	Whitebrowed Robin *E. leucophrys*	V/Re	ML	T	N K – L
392	Central Bearded Scrub Robin *E. barbata*	F/Re	M	CN	N K – –
393	Bearded Robin *E. quadrivirgata*	F/Re	ML	T	– – – –
394	Collared Palm Thrush *Cichladusa arquata*	C/Re	ML	T	– – Li L
395	Cholo Alethe *Alethe choloensis*	ULRe	M	S	– – – –
396	Whitebreasted Alethe *A. fuelleborni*	ULRe	H	N	N – – –
397	Oliveflanked Robin *A. anomala*	FLRe	H	NS	N – – –
398	Sharpe's Akalat *Sheppardia sharpei*	ULRe	H	N	N – – –
399	Gunning's Robin *S. gunningi*	ULRe	ML	N	– – – –
400	Starred Robin *Pogonocichla stellata*	C/Re	HM	T	N – – –
401	Natal Robin *Cossypha natalensis*	C/Re	ML	T	N – Li L
402	Cape Robin *C. caffra*	C/Re	HM	T	N – – –
403	Heuglin's Robin *C. heuglini*	V/Re	ML	T	N K Li L
404	Spot-throat Modulatrix *Modulatrix stictigula*	RLRe	H	N	– – – –
405	Thrush Nightingale *Luscinia luscinia*	FSVi	ML	T	– K – L
406	Mountain Thrush *Turdus abyssinicus*	ULRe	H	NS	N – – –
407	Kurrichane Thrush *T. libonyana*	V/Re	ML	T	N K Li L
408	Spotted Thrush *T. fischeri*	RLRe	M	S	– – – –
409	Groundscraper Thrush *T. litsitsirupa*	U/Re	M	NC	– K – –
410	Orange Thrush *T. gurneyi*	F/Re	HM	T	N – – –

Local.	Habitat	Comments
Sv	Th	*See page 14.*
	Br, Ac	**p. 328**
Vi, Dz	Br, Th	*See page 14.*
Sv, Mj	Th, Ef	Occasionally in riparian evergreen forest. **p. 328**
Ka	Th	Wherever there are Borassus or Hyphaene palms. **p. 330**
Tm, Mj	Ef	*See page 14.*
Mi, Vi	Ef	Recorded only west of the Rift from the Viphya northwards in the ground stratum of montane and submontane evergreen forest. **p. 322**
Vi, Mj	Ef	*See page 14.*
Vi	Ef	*See page 14.*
Nk	Ef	Recorded in riparian evergreen forest around Mzuzu to the lowland evergreen forests near Nkhata Bay. **p. 326**
Vi, Tm	Ef	Any evergreen forest; descends to lower altitudes in winter. **p. 326**
Nk	Th, Ef	Ground stratum of submontane and riparian evergreen forest. **p. 328**
Za, Mj	Bb	Habitat usually bracken-brier, occasionally on the edges of montane evergreen forest. **p. 324**
	*	Very common in gardens and in riparian evergreen forest. **p. 324**
Mi	Ef	*See page 14.*
Lm, Sv	Ac, Th	A skulking species more often heard than seen. **p. 332**
Tm, Mj	Ef	Not illustrated. In the field this species is practically identical to the montane (dark) race of the Olive Thrush. **p. 312**
	Br, Ac	**p. 312**
Tm, Mj	Ef	Only recorded east of the Rift in a few submontane evergreen forests where it inhabits the ground stratum. **p. 312**
Ld	Br, Ac	Found in Brachystegia and Acacia woodland with an open understory. **p. 312**
Za, Mj	Ef	Inhabits the ground stratum of montane and submontane evergreen forest. **p. 312**

BOM	Family / species	Stat.	Al.	Ra.	Nat. Park
	Warblers SYLVIIDAE				
411	African Sedge Warbler *Bradypterus baboecala*	F/Re	ML	T	N – Li –
412	Eastern Forest Scrub Warbler *B. mariae*	C/Re	HM	T	N – – –
413	Longtailed Forest Scrub Warbler *B. cinnamomeus*	FLRe	H	NS	N – – –
414	Broadtailed Warbler *Schoenicola brevirostris*	U/Re	M	T	N – – –
415	River Warbler *Locustella fluviatilis*	RSVi	ML	S	– – – –
416	European Sedge Warbler *Acrocephalus schoenobaenus*	F/Re	ML	T	N – – –
417	European Marsh Warbler *A. palustris*	USVi	ML	T	– K – L
418	European Reed Warbler *A. scirpaceus*	RSVi	ML	CS	– – – –
419	Great Reed Warbler *A. arundinaceus*	FSVi	ML	CS	– K – L
420	Basra Reed Warbler *A. griseldis*	USVi	L	S	– – – –
421	African Marsh Warbler *A. baeticatus*	F/Re	ML	T	– – Li –
422	Cape Reed Warbler *A. gracilirostris*	F/Re	ML	T	– K – L
423	Yellow Warbler *Chloropeta natalensis*	F/Re	HM	T	N – Li –
424	Yellow Mountain Warbler *C. similis*	F/Re	H	N	N – – –
425	Moustached Warbler *Melocichla mentalis*	F/Re	ML	T	– K – L
426	Icterine Warbler *Hippolais icterina*	USVi	ML	T	– K Li –
427	Olivetree Warbler *H. olivetorum*	USVi	ML	S	– – Li –
428	Garden Warbler *Sylvia borin*	CSVi	A	T	N K Li L
429	European Blackcap *S. atricapilla*	RSVi	HM	T	N – – –
430	Whitethroat *S. communis*	USVi	ML	T	N – – –
430A	European Barred Warbler *S. nisoria*	RSVi	L	S	– – – –
431	Brown Warbler *Parisoma lugens*	FLRe	HM	NC	N – – –

Local.	Habitat	Comments
Mp, Em	Ma	Inhabits the lower growth of dense swampy vegetation or reedbeds near water. **p. 336**
De, Tm	Ef	*See page 16.*
Mj	Bb	*See page 16.*
Vi, De	Gl	Usually in rank grass, occasionally in Bango reeds near streams. **p. 334**
Sv	Th, Gl, Ma	Often away from water. **p. 334**
Cd, Sr	Ma	Generally found in taller reeds than the African Sedge Warbler. **p. 336**
Sv	Th	In Africa not necessarily found near marsh, usually in woody vegetation with long grass at the edge of thicket. **p. 336**
Lm, Sv	Th, Gl	Not normally near reeds, though may occur in thickets at the edge of wet areas. **p. 336**
Sr	Gl, Ma	Similar in habitat to the African Sedge Warbler, but is less skulking and very vocal. **p. 338**
Sv	Th, Gl, Ma	Often in dry thickets away from water. **p. 338**
Lc, Em	Gl, Ma	Normally in marsh and reedbeds but moves into long rank grass with small bushes during the rains. **p. 336**
Lc, Em	Ma	Inhabits marshes and reedbeds. **p. 336**
Za, Mj	Bb, Gl	Often in rank growth along drainage lines. **p. 338**
	Bb	*See page 16.*
Vi, Za	Bb, Gl	Preferred habitat is long rank grass with bushes. **p. 348**
Ld	Br, Ac	In summer regularly seen in the Thyolo district. **p. 332**
Ld, Sv	Th, Br, Ac	**p. 332**
	Br, Ac, Ef	Feeds in any woodland including the edge of evergreen forest and in gardens. **p. 332**
Vi, Za	Br, Ef	*See page 16.*
Za, Bd	Br, Ac, Th	**p. 334**
Sv	Th	*See page 16.*
De	Ac	*See page 16.*

BOM	Family / species	Stat.	Al.	Ra.	Nat. Park
432	Willow Warbler *Phylloscopus trochilus*	VSVi	A	T	N K Li L
433	Yellowthroated Warbler *Seicercus ruficapillus*	F/Re	HM	T	N – – –
434	Tawnyflanked Prinia *Prinia subflava*	C/Re	ML	T	N K Li L
435	Redwinged Warbler *Heliolais erythroptera*	F/Re	ML	T	N K – L
436	Barthroated Apalis *Apalis thoracica*	C/Re	HM	T	N – – –
436A	Rudd's Apalis *A. ruddi*	RLRe	L	S	– – – L
437	Whitewinged Apalis *A. chariessa*	RLRe	M	S	– – – –
438	Yellowbreasted Apalis *A. flavida*	C/Re	ML	T	N – Li L
439	Chestnut-throated Apalis *A. porphyrolaema*	F/Re	HM	NC	N – – –
440	Brownheaded Apalis *A. cinerea*	ULRe	H	N	N – – –
441	Blackheaded Apalis *A. melanocephala*	F/Re	M	S	– – – –
442	Bleating Bush Warbler *Camaroptera brachyura*	V/Re	ML	T	N K – L
443	Stierling's Barred Warbler *C. stierlingi*	F/Re	M	T	N K – –
445	Yellowbellied Eremomela *Eremomela icteropygialis*	F/Re	ML	T	N K – L
446	Greencapped Eremomela *E. scotops*	C/Re	ML	T	N K Li L
447	Burntnecked Eremomela *E. usticollis*	U/Re	L	CS	– – Li –
448	Redfaced Crombec *Sylvietta whytii*	C/Re	M	T	– – – –
449	Redcapped Crombec *S. ruficapilla*	F/Re	M	NC	N K – –
450	Longbilled Crombec *S. rufescens*	V/Re	ML	T	N K Li L
451	Yellowbreasted Hyliota *Hyliota flavigaster*	F/Re	M	T	N K – –
452	Mashona Hyliota *H. australis*	F/Re	M	CS	– – – –
453	Redfaced Cisticola *Cisticola erythrops*	C/Re	ML	T	N K Li L

Local.	Habitat	Comments
	*	Canopy of any woodland or the edge of evergreen forest. **p. 332**
Za, Tm	Ef	Mid-stratum of montane or submontane evergreen forest. ***See page 18***; **p. 344**
	Br, Gl	**p. 358**
Mj	Br, Gl	Usually in thicker rank growth than previous species and rarely alongside it. **p. 360**
De, Mj	Ef, Bb	***See page 18***; **p. 340**
Sv	Th	Confined to the lower Shire valley in and near Lengwe N.P. **p. 340**
Bd, Tm	Ef	***See page 18.***
	*	Any woodland, thicket or edge of riparian evergreen forest. **p. 340**
Mi	Ef	***See page 18.***
Mi	Ef	***See page 18.***
Za, Tm	Ef	Only east of the Rift, in the canopy of submontane evergreen forest **p. 340**
	*	Ground stratum of any woodland, thicket, riparian or submontane evergreen forest. **p. 346**
Dz, Ph	Br	A hybrid between this species and the Plain Bush Warbler is known from Chitipa. **p. 346**
Dz, Ph	Br, Ac	Often in Brachystegia or Acacia woodland bird parties. **p. 344**
	Br	Occasionally alongside the previous species. **p. 344**
	Ac	More or less confined to Acacia woodland. Quite common around Salima. **p. 344**
Za, Bd	Br	**p. 342**
Ch, Dz	Br	**p. 342**
	Mo, Ac	**p. 342**
Dz, Ph	Br	This and the next species have been recorded together at Mchinji, Dzalanyama and Phirilongwe. **p. 360**
Dz, Ph	Br	**p. 360**
Ll	Gl	Usually in rank grass near streams. **p. 356**

BOM	Family / species	Stat.	Al.	Ra.	Nat. Park
454	Singing Cisticola *C. cantans*	C/Re	ML	T	N K – –
455	Trilling Cisticola *C. woosnami*	U/Re	HM	N	N – – –
456	Mountain Cisticola *C. hunteri*	FLRe	H	N	N – – –
457	Lazy Cisticola *C. aberrans*	F/Re	HM	T	N K – –
458	Rattling Cisticola *C. chiniana*	C/Re	ML	T	– K Li L
459	Tinkling Cisticola *C. rufilata*	U/Re	M	NC	– K – –
460	Wailing Cisticola *C. lais*	C/Re	H	T	N – – –
461	Churring Cisticola *C. njombe*	FLRe	H	N	N – – –
462	Blackbacked Cisticola *C. galactotes*	C/Re	ML	T	– K Li –
463	Croaking Cisticola *C. natalensis*	C/Re	ML	T	N K Li L
464	Neddicky *C. fulvicapilla*	C/Re	ML	T	N K Li L
465	Shortwinged Cisticola *C. brachyptera*	F/Re	ML	T	N K – L
466	Fantailed Cisticola *C. juncidis*	C/Re	ML	T	– K – –
467	Ayres' Cisticola *C. ayresii*	FLRe	H	N	N – – –
	Flycatchers MUSCICAPIDAE				
468	Spotted Flycatcher *Muscicapa striata*	CSVi	A	T	N K Li L
469	Collared Flycatcher *Ficedula albicollis*	USVi	M	T	N K – –
470	Dusky Flycatcher *Muscicapa adusta*	C/Re	HM	T	N – Li L
471	Bluegrey Flycatcher *M. caerulescens*	F/Re	ML	T	N K Li L
472	Boehm's Flycatcher *Myopornis boehmi*	F/Re	M	T	N K – –
473	Fantailed Flycatcher *Myioparus plumbeus*	F/Re	ML	T	N K Li L
474	Slaty Flycatcher *Melaenornis chocolatina*	F/Re	HM	NC	N – – –

Local.	Habitat	Comments
Za, Bd	Bb, Gl	Similar habitat to that of the Redfaced Cisticola but normally away from streams. **p. 352**
Vi	Br	*See page 20.*
Mi	Bb, Gl	*See page 20.*
Ph	Br	Usually where there are rocks in Brachystegia woodland. **p. 356**
Lm, Sv	Ac	Inhabits abandoned cultivations or rank grass under Acacia and to a lesser degree Brachystegia woodland. **p. 354**
De	Br	Habitat as for the Rattling Cisticola but only in Brachystegia woodland. **p. 354**
De, Mj	Bb, Gs	Only in montane grassland or bracken-brier. **p. 354**
	Bb, Gl	*See page 20.*
Mp, Lc	Ma	Reeds near marshes or streams. **p. 354**
	Gs	Short grass under very sparse Brachystegia woodland or shrubs. **p. 356**
Dz, Bd	Br, Mo	Short grass in Brachystegia or Mopane woodland. **p. 352**
Vi, Bd	Gs	Grassy clearings in any open or semi-open country. **p. 352**
Lc, Cd	Gs, Dw	Only in open areas of short wet grass. Sings aerially. **p. 350**
	Gs	Confined to montane grassland on the Nyika Plateau. **p. 350**
*		Any woodland habitat. **p. 362**
Vi	Br	Has been recorded regularly around Mzuzu. **p. 360**
	Br, Ef	Brachystegia woodland and the edges of any evergreen forest. **p. 362**
Bd	Br, Ef, Th	Brachystegia woodland, thicket or the fringes of riparian evergreen forest. **p. 362**
Dz	Br	*See page 20.*
Sv	Br, Ac, Th	**p. 362**
Mi, De	Ef	*See page 20.*

BOM	Family / species	Stat.	Al.	Ra.	Nat. Park
475	Black Flycatcher *M. pammelaina*	C/Re	ML	T	N K Li L
476	Mousecoloured Flycatcher *M. pallidus*	F/Re	ML	T	N K Li L
477	Vanga Flycatcher *Bias musicus*	RLRe	L	S	– – – L
478	Cape Batis *Batis capensis*	C/Re	HM	T	N – – –
479	Chinspot Batis *B. molitor*	V/Re	A	T	N K Li L
480	Mozambique Batis *B. soror*	V/Re	ML	S	– – – –
481	Woodward's Batis *B. fratrum*	ULRe	L	S	– – – L
482	Wattle-eyed Flycatcher *Platysteira peltata*	C/Re	ML	T	– – Li L
483	Livingstone's Flycatcher *Erythrocercus livingstonei*	F/Re	L	CS	– – Li L
484	Whitetailed Blue Flycatcher *Elminia albicauda*	F/Re	HM	NC	N – – –
485	Bluemantled Flycatcher *Trochocercus cyanomelas*	U/Re	ML	T	– – – L
486	Whitetailed Flycatcher *T. albonotatus*	C/Re	HM	T	N – – –
487	Paradise Flycatcher *Terpsiphone viridis*	CSRe	ML	T	N K Li L
	Tchagras and bush shrikes MALACONOTIDAE				
488	Brubru *Nilaus afer*	F/Re	ML	T	N K Li L
489	Puffback *Dryoscopus cubla*	V/Re	ML	T	N K Li L
490	Marsh Tchagra *Tchagra minuta*	U/Re	ML	T	N – – –
491	Threestreaked Tchagra *T. australis*	C/Re	ML	T	N K Li L
492	Blackcrowned Tchagra *T. senegala*	C/Re	A	T	N K Li L
493	Southern Boubou *Laniarius ferrugineus*	C/Re	A	T	N K Li L
494	Fülleborn's Black Boubou *L. fuelleborni*	F/Re	H	N	N – – –
495	Orangebreasted Bush Shrike *Telophorus sulfureopectus*	C/Re	ML	T	N K Li L

Local.	Habitat	Comments
	Br, Mo, Ac	**p. 296**
Ch	Br, Mo	**p. 362**
Sv	Th	Confined to the Shire valley near Lengwe N.P. **p. 364**
Vi, Tm	Ef	*See page 22;* **p. 366**
	Br, Mo, Ac	Common west of the Rift; east found only in the Rift Valley floor from Liwonde N.P. to bottom of the eastern escarpment. **p. 366**
Bd, Mj	Br	Recorded in Brachystegia woodland east of the Rift. **p. 366**
Sv	Th	Only in the deciduous thickets of the lower Shire valley and in the lowland evergreen forest of the Malawi Hills. **p. 366**
Za, Tm	Th, Ef	Ground stratum of submontane and riparian evergreen forest. **p. 368**
Ll, Sv	Th, Ef	In the central region occurs in riparian evergreen forest. **p. 368**
Vi, Dz	Br, Ef	*See page 20.*
Tm, Mj	Th, Ef	Found in submontane and riparian evergreen forest. **p. 368**
Vi, Tm	Ef	Canopy and mid-stratum of montane and submontane evergreen forest. **p. 368**
	*	Two races occur in Malawi: *T.v. violacea* breeds and *T.v. granti* is a winter visitor. **p. 368**
Ch, Ph	Br, Ac	**p. 372**
	*	Habitat includes all evergreen forest except montane. **p. 372**
	Bb, Gl	Inhabits rank growth in open country. Has been seen near the Ntchisi F.R. and in the Thyolo district. **p. 376**
	Gl	Inhabits rank growth in any woodland habitat. **p. 376**
	Bb, Gl	Habitat similar to that of previous species, but often in moister areas. **p. 376**
	*	Common in gardens and all types of evergreen forest. **p. 374**
Mi, Vi	Ef	*See page 22.*
	Ac, Th, Ef	Occasionally in riparian evergreen forest. **p. 378**

BOM	Family / species	Stat.	Al.	Ra.	Nat. Park
496	Blackfronted Bush Shrike *T. nigrifrons*	F/Re	HM	NS	N – – –
497	Olive Bush Shrike *T. olivaceus*	ULRe	H	CS	– – – –
498	Greyheaded Bush Shrike *Melaconotus blanchoti*	F/Re	ML	T	N K Li L
499	Gorgeous Bush Shrike *Telophorus quadricolor*	RLRe	L	S	– – – L
	Wagtails, pipits and longclaws MOTACILLIDAE				
500	Yellow Wagtail *Motacilla flava*	CSVi	ML	T	N – Li L
501	Longtailed Wagtail *M. clara*	F/Re	ML	T	N – – –
502	Grey Wagtail *M. cinerea*	RSVi	M	S	– – – –
503	African Pied Wagtail *M. aguimp*	A/Re	ML	T	N K Li L
504	White Wagtail *M. alba*	RSVi	M	S	– – – –
505	Grassveld Pipit *Anthus cinnamomeus*	V/Re	A	T	N K Li L
506	Plainbacked Pipit *A. leucophrys*	U/Re	ML	T	– K – –
507	Buffy Pipit *A. vaalensis*	UWVi	A	T	N K – –
508	Wood Pipit *A. nyassae*	F/Re	HM	T	– K – –
508A	Jackson's Pipit *A. latistriatus*	ULRe	HM	NC	N – – –
509	Bushveld Pipit *A. caffer*	R/Re	M	C	– – – –
510	Tree Pipit *A. trivialis*	FSVi	HM	T	N – – –
511	Striped Pipit *A. lineiventris*	F/Re	M	T	N K – –
512	Yellowthroated Longclaw *Macronyx croceus*	C/Re	ML	T	– K Li L
513	Pinkthroated Longclaw *M. ameliae*	ULRe	M	NC	– – – –
	Shrikes LANIIDAE				
514	Redbacked Shrike *Lanius collurio*	CSVi	A	T	N K Li L

Local.	Habitat	Comments
Mi, Tm	Ef	Canopy of montane and submontane evergreen forest. **p. 378**
Za, Mj	Ef	Recorded only on Zomba and Mulanje Plateaux in the canopy of montane evergreen forest, sometimes bracken-brier. **p. 378**
	*	Any woodland or thicket. **p. 380**
	Th	In recent years apparently absent from Lengwe N.P., may still survive on the Malawi Hills F.R. **p. 378**
Mp, Lc	Gs	Common in large areas of short grass or bare ground. **p. 292**
Za, Mj	Ri	Confined to rocky streams and rivers. **p. 294**
Za	Ri	Habitat as for Longtailed Wagtail, but much less common. **p. 294**
	*	Usually near human habitation. **p. 294**
	Gs	*See page 10.*
	Gs	**p. 288**
Lc, Cd	Gs	This and the next species are difficult to differentiate in the field. **p. 288**
Ld, Lc	Gs	Common in the Lilongwe district during the dry season. **p. 288**
Vw, Za	Br	*See page 10.*
Mi, De	Gs	*See page 10.*
	Br	No recent records. **p. 290**
De, Mj	Br, Bb, Gs	**p. 290**
Dz, Bd	Br, Ro	Found where there are rocks under Brachystegia woodland. Flies to the mid-stratum when flushed. **p. 290**
Be, Bd	Gl, Gs, Dw	Common on the edges of dambos where there are bushes to perch on. **p. 292**
Ld, Be	Dw	Inhabits grass dambos without bushes and is found only in the central region between Kasungu and Dedza. **p. 290**
	*	**p. 370**

BOM	Family / species	Stat.	Al.	Ra.	Nat. Park
514A	Redtailed Shrike *L. isabellinus*	RSVi	M	N	N – – –
515	Lesser Grey Shrike *L. minor*	USVi	A	T	N K – –
516	Longtailed Shrike *Corvinella melanoleuca*	R/Va	ML	T	– – – –
517	Fiscal Shrike *Lanius collaris*	V/Re	A	T	N K Li –
518	Souza's Shrike *L. souzae*	U/Re	M	T	N K – –
	Helmetshrikes PRIONOPIDAE				
519	White Helmetshrike *Prionops plumatus*	C/Re	ML	T	N K Li L
520	Redbilled Helmetshrike *P. retzii*	C/Re	A	T	N K Li L
	Starlings STURNIDAE				
521	Waller's Redwinged Starling *Onychognathus walleri*	ULRe	H	N	N – – –
522	Redwinged Starling *O. morio*	C/Re	A	T	N K Li L
523	Slenderbilled Redwinged Starling *O. tenuirostris*	ULRe	H	N	N – – –
524	Lesser Blue-eared Glossy Starling *Lamprotornis chloropterus*	C/Re	ML	T	N K Li L
525	Greater Blue-eared Glossy Starling *L. chalybaeus*	C/Re	ML	T	– K Li L
526	Longtailed Glossy Starling *L. mevesii*	CL/Re	M	S	– – Li –
527	Plumcoloured Starling *Cinnyricinclus leucogaster*	CSRe	A	T	N K Li L
528	Whitewinged Babbling Starling *Neocichla gutturalis*	ULRe	M	N	– – – –
529	Wattled Starling *Creatophora cinerea*	U/Re	A	T	N K Li –
	Oxpeckers BUPHAGIDAE				
530	Yellowbilled Oxpecker *Buphagus africanus*	U/Re	ML	T	– K Li L
531	Redbilled Oxpecker *B. erythrorhynchus*	U/Re	ML	T	– K Li L
	Sunbirds NECTARINIIDAE				
532	Red and Blue Sunbird *Anthreptes anchietae*	F/Re	M	NC	N K – –

Local.	Habitat	Comments
	Bb	*See page 22.*
Ld, Bd	*	Much less common than the Redbacked Shrike. **p. 370**
Sv	Ac	There are a few scattered records of this species, mostly from the lower Shire valley. **p. 370**
Bd	Br, Mo, Ac	Perches on telephone wires. **p. 372**
Dz, Za	Br	A sparse, solitary species found in Brachystegia woodland. **p. 374**
	Br, Mo, Ac	**p. 380**
	*	Usually in richer vegetation than the previous species, including thicket and riparian evergreen forest. **p. 380**
Mi	Ef	*See page 22.*
	Ro	Wanders locally away from rocky hills. **p. 382**
	Ef	*See page 22.*
Ld, Bd	Br, Ac	Difficult to tell from the next species but the immatures are chestnut below and the call is tuneful. **p. 386**
Ka	Mo, Ac	Call a harsh disyllic churr. Less common at mid-altitudes than the previous species. **p. 386**
Ll	Mo, Ac	Confined to the southern end of Lake Malawi, Lake Malombe and Liwonde N.P. **p.384**
	*	Present in summer only. **p. 384**
Vw	Br	*See page 22.*
Ka, Lc,	Br, Mo, Ac	All recent records are of birds in non-breeding plumage; appears to be quite common around Karonga. **p. 382**
	Br, Mo, Ac	This and the next species are more or less confined to the national parks where big game survives. **p. 388**
	Br, Mo, Ac	**p. 388**
Ch, Dz	Br	*See page 24.*

BOM	Family / species	Stat.	Al.	Ra.	Nat. Park
533	Violetbacked Sunbird *A. longuemarei*	F/Re	ML	T	N K –
534	Collared Sunbird *A. collaris*	V/Re	ML	T	N – Li
535	Olive Sunbird *Nectarinia olivacea*	C/Re	M	T	N – –
536	Greenheaded Sunbird *N. verticalis*	U/Re	M	N	N – –
537	Black Sunbird *N. amethystina*	C/Re	ML	T	N K Li
538	Scarletchested Sunbird *N. senegalensis*	C/Re	ML	T	N K Li
539	Whitebellied Sunbird *N. talatala*	C/Re	M	T	– – Li
539A	Oustalet's Sunbird *N. oustaleti*	U/Re	M	C	– K –
540	Yellowbellied Sunbird *N. venusta*	C/Re	A	T	N K Li
541	Greater Doublecollared Sunbird *N. afra*	ULRe	H	N	N – –
542	Miombo Doublecollared Sunbird *N. manoensis*	C/Re	HM	T	N K –
543	Eastern Doublecollared Sunbird *N. mediocris*	C/Re	H	T	N – –
544	Shelley's Sunbird *N. shelleyi*	U/Re	ML	T	– – –
545	Purplebanded Sunbird *N. bifasciata*	F/Re	ML	T	– K Li L
546	Coppery Sunbird *N. cuprea*	U/Re	ML	T	– K – L
546A	Grey Sunbird *N. veroxii*	RLRe	L	S	– – – L
547	Malachite Sunbird *N. famosa*	F/Re	H	N	N – –
548	Redtufted Malachite Sunbird *N. johnstoni*	ULRe	H	N	N – –
549	Bronze Sunbird *N. kilimensis*	F/Re	H	T	N – –
	White-eyes ZOSTEROPIDAE				
550	Yellow White-eye *Zosterops senegalensis*	C/Re	A	T	N K Li L

Local.	Habitat	Comments
Ch, Dz	Br	A quiet species, sometimes in mixed Brachystegia bird parties. Common north of the Nyika. **p. 398**
	*	Any tree habitat, including edges of submontane and riparian evergreen forest. **p. 394**
Nk, Tm	Ef, Th	Young birds have orange throats; the pectoral patch is yellow. Inhabits submontane and riparian evergreen forest. **p. 400**
Mi	Ef	***See page 24.***
Za, Bd	Br, Ac	Common in rich Brachystegia, rarely in Acacia woodland. Occasionally with the next species. **p. 396**
Ll	Br, Mo, Ac	Usually in drier areas than the Black Sunbird. **p. 396**
Ll, Sv	Th, Mo, Ac	Anyone visiting the Chitipa district should keep an eye open for the very similar Oustalet's Sunbird, the next species. **p. 394**
	Br	***See page 24.***
	*	**p. 394**
	Bb, Gs	**p. 392**
Za, Mj	Br, Bb	The local race has less blue on the upper tail coverts. More common in bracken and brier than in Brachystegia woodland. **p. 392**
De, Mj	Ef, Bb	***See page 24.***
De, Ph	Br	More often solitary than in Brachystegia bird parties. **p. 392**
Dz, Sv	Ac, Th	**p. 398**
Ld, Sv	Br, Ac	**p. 390**
Sv	Th	Confined to the lower Shire valley in and near Lengwe N.P. **p. 400**
Mi, Vi	Bb, Gs	Feeds on flowering Protea bushes. **p. 390**
	Bb, Gs	***See page 24.***
Vi, De	Bb	Only west of the Rift; particularly fond of flowering Leonotis (nettle) and Loranthus (mistletoe) plants. **p. 390**
	*	Inhabits any tree habitat including evergreen forest. **p. 402**

BOM	Family / species	Stat.	Al.	Ra.	Nat. Park
	Weavers and queleas PLOCEIDAE				
551	Thickbilled Weaver *Amblyospiza albifrons*	C/Re	ML	T	– – Li –
552	Baglafecht Weaver *Ploceus baglafecht*	ULRe	H	N	N – – –
553	Bertram's Weaver *P. bertrandi*	F/Re	HM	T	N – – –
554	Yellow Weaver *P. subaureus*	C/Re	L	T	– K Li –
555	Golden Weaver *P. xanthops*	C/Re	ML	T	N – – –
556	Brownthroated Weaver *P. xanthopterus*	C/Re	L	T	– – Li L
557	Lesser Masked Weaver *P. intermedius*	C/Re	ML	T	– – Li L
558	Masked Weaver *P. velatus*	C/Re	ML	T	N K Li L
559	Spottedbacked Weaver *P. cucullatus*	C/Re	ML	T	– K – L
560	Forest Weaver *P. bicolor*	F/Re	ML	CS	– – – L
561	Spectacled Weaver *P. ocularis*	C/Re	ML	T	N K Li L
562	Oliveheaded Weaver *P. olivaceiceps*	U/Re	M	T	– – – –
563	Redheaded Weaver *Anaplectes rubriceps*	F/Re	ML	T	N K Li L
564	Cardinal Quelea *Quelea cardinalis*	R/Va	C	M	– – – –
565	Redheaded Quelea *Q. erythrops*	USRe	ML	T	– – Li L
566	Redbilled Quelea *Q. quelea*	V/Re	ML	T	– K Li L
567	Red Bishop *Euplectes orix*	V/Re	ML	T	– – Li L
568	Firecrowned Bishop *E. hordeaceus*	C/Re	ML	T	N – Li L
569	Yellowrumped Widow *E. capensis*	V/Re	ML	T	N K Li L
570	Yellowbacked Widow *E. macrourus*	F/Re	M	NC	– K – –
571	Redshouldered Widow *E. axillaris*	F/Re	ML	T	– – Li L
572	Mountain Marsh Widow *E. psammocromius*	FLRe	H	N	N – – –

Local.	Habitat	Comments
LI, Sv	Ma	Sometimes feeds on fruiting trees in submontane riparian evergreen forest. **p. 410**
	Bb	*See page 26.*
Za, Tm	Bb	*See page 26.*
LI, Sv	Ma	Generally in larger numbers and at lower altitudes than the next species. **p.410**
Ld, Bd	Gl	Found in small groups, often in rank grass by streams. **p. 410**
LI, Sv	Ma	Nests in large colonies. **p. 410**
LI, Sv	Ac, Ma	Another nester in very large colonies. **p. 412**
LI, Sv	Ac	Moves into other habitats, especially near houses. **p. 412**
LI, Sv	Ac	Often near water. **p. 412**
Za, Tm	Ef, Th	Inhabits the mid-stratum and canopy of submontane and riparian evergreen forest. **p. 408**
LI	Gl	Pairs or small groups occur in rank growth near streams. **p. 410**
Vi, Dz	Br	Often solitary but may be found in mixed Brachystegia bird parties. **p. 408**
Dz, Ph	Ac, Br	Usually in pairs or one male with a few females. **p. 412**
Ld	Gl	*See page 26.*
Lc, LI	Gl	Much less common than the Redbilled Quelea; present in summer only. **p. 402**
LI, Sv	Ac, Gl	Not found in the huge flocks that occur in other parts of Africa. **p. 404**
LI, Sv	Ac, Gl, Ma	Generally in lower, drier areas than the Firecrowned Bishop. **p. 416**
Ld, Bd	Gl	In any lightly wooded habitat where rank growth occurs. Often away from water, sometimes with Red Bishops. **p. 416**
	*	**p. 418**
Dz, Be	Dw	This species is found above 900 m. **p. 418**
Lc, Sv	Dw, Ma	Recorded below 900 m. **p. 416**
	Bb	*See page 26.*

BOM	Family / species	Stat.	Al.	Ra.	Nat. Park
573	Whitewinged Widow *E. albonotatus*	F/Re	ML	T	N – Li L
574	Redcollared Widow *E. ardens*	F/Re	A	T	N K Li –
575	Cuckoo Finch *Anomalospiza imberbis*	U/Re	A	T	– – – L
576	Whitebrowed Sparrow-weaver *Plocepasser mahali*	C/Re	ML	CS	– – Li L
577	Chestnutmantled Sparrow-weaver *P. rufocapulatus*	ULRe	M	C	– K – –
578	House Sparrow *Passer domesticus*	C/Re	ML	T	– K – –
579	Greyheaded Sparrow *P. griseus*	V/Re	ML	T	– K Li L
580	Yellowthroated Sparrow *Petronia superciliaris*	V/Re	A	T	N K Li L
	Whydahs and widowfinches VIDUIDAE				
581	Pintailed Whydah *Vidua macroura*	V/Re	ML	T	– K Li L
582	Purple Widowfinch *V. purpurascens*	F/Re	ML	T	– – – L
583	Black Widowfinch *V. funerea*	C/Re	M	T	N K – L
584	Steelblue Widowfinch *V. chalybeata*	C/Re	ML	T	– – Li L
585	Paradise Whydah *V. paradisea*	C/Re	ML	T	N K Li L
586	Broadtailed Paradise Whydah *V. obtusa*	F/Re	ML	T	N K Li L
	Pytilias, waxbills, mannikins, etc. ESTRILDIDAE				
587	Goldenbacked Pytilia *Pytilia afra*	F/Re	ML	T	N K Li L
588	Melba Finch *P. melba*	C/Re	ML	T	– K Li L
589	Green Twinspot *Mandingoa nitidula*	U/Re	ML	T	N – – L
590	Redfaced Crimsonwing *Cryptospiza reichenowii*	F/Re	HM	T	N – – –
591	Nyasa Seedcracker *Pyrenestes minor*	U/Re	HM	T	– – – –
592	Redthroated Twinspot *Hypargos niveoguttatus*	C/Re	ML	T	N – Li L
593	Redbilled Firefinch *Lagonosticta senegala*	V/Re	ML	T	– K Li L

96

Local.	Habitat	Comments
Ll, Sv	Br, Gl	**p. 416**
Ld, Bd	Br, Bb, Gl	Some individuals lack the red collar. **p. 416**
Be, Cd	Gs, Dw	A sparse species found in small groups in the bushy margins of grassland. **p. 430**
Ll, Sv	Mo, Ac	Very common in the Rift from the southern and of Lake Malawi to the lower Shire valley. **p. 406**
	Br	*See page 26.*
Ld, Bd	*	Has probably spread throughout the country. Common near human habitation. **p. 404**
	Br	Also found near human habitation. **p. 404**
	Br, Mo, Ac	**p. 404**
	Br, Gl, Gs	**p. 432**
Ll, Sv	Gl	Found at low altitudes where its host, the Jameson's Firefinch, occurs. **p. 434**
Ld, Bd	Br, Gl	Usually at mid-altitude, where the Bluebilled Firefinch is found. **p. 434**
Ll	*	Wherever Redbilled Firefinches occur. **p. 434**
Ll, Lc	Mo, Ac	Occurs in much drier areas than the Broadtailed Paradise Whydah. **p. 432**
Dz, Ph	Br	Very occasionally alongside the previous species. **p. 434**
Dz, Ph	Br, Th	Sometimes near the next species. **p. 420**
Ll	Br, Mo, Ac	Usually in moister places than the Goldenbacked Pytilia. **p. 420**
Mj	Th, Ef	Ground stratum of submontane and riparian evergreen forest, occasionally in the canopy when suitable trees are seeding. **p. 424**
Tm, Mj	Ef	Inhabits the ground stratum of montane and submontane evergreen forest. **p. 420**
Dz	Bb, Gl	Occasionally in rank growth on the edges of riparian evergreen forest. Recorded in the Namizimu F.R. **p. 420**
	Th, Ef	A common garden bird, also in the ground stratum of submontane and riparian evergreen forest. **p. 424**
Ll	Gl	Always near human habitation. **p. 422**

BOM	Family / species	Stat.	Al.	Ra.	Nat. Park
594	Bluebilled Firefinch *L. rubricata*	V/Re	HM	T	N K Li L
595	Jameson's Firefinch *L. rhodopareia*	C/Re	ML	T	– K Li L
596	Blue Waxbill *Uraeginthus angolensis*	A/Re	ML	T	N K Li L
597	Grey Waxbill *Estrilda perreini*	RLRe	ML	T	N – – –
598	East African Swee *E. quartinia*	C/Re	HM	T	N – – –
599	Crimsonrumped Waxbill *E. rhodopyga*	ULRe	L	N	– – – –
600	Common Waxbill *E. astrild*	C/Re	ML	T	N K Li L
601	Orangebreasted Waxbill *Sporaeginthus subflavus*	F/Re	ML	T	N – Li L
602	Quail Finch *Ortygospiza atricollis*	U/Re	M	T	– – – –
603	Locust Finch *O. locustella*	F/Re	M	T	– K Li –
604	Bronze Mannikin *Spermestes cucullatus*	A/Re	ML	T	N K Li L
605	Redbacked Mannikin *S. bicolor*	C/Re	ML	T	N – Li L
606	Pied Mannikin *S. fringilloides*	U/Re	ML	T	– – Li –
607	Cutthroat Finch *Amadina fasciata*	C/Re	ML	CS	– – Li L
	Buntings, canaries and seedeaters FRINGILLIDAE				
608	Cabanis's Bunting *Emberiza cabanisi*	C/Re	A	T	N K – –
609	Goldenbreasted Bunting *E. flaviventris*	F/Re	ML	T	N K Li L
610	Rock Bunting *E. tahapisi*	C/Re	A	T	N K Li L
611	Cape Bunting *E. capensis*	U/Re	HM	T	– K – –
612	Yelloweyed Canary *Serinus mozambicus*	A/Re	ML	T	N K Li L
613	Lemonbreasted Canary *S. citrinipectus*	ULRe	L	S	– – – L
614	Bully Canary *S. sulphuratus*	F/Re	A	T	N K Li L

Local.	Habitat	Comments
Mi, Vi	Br, Gl	More likely at higher altitudes than the Jameson's Firefinch. **p. 422**
Ll, Sv	Th, Gl	Not usually found alongside the previous species. **p. 422**
	Ac, Th, Gl	**p. 426**
Sv	Ef, Gl	Recently recorded on the edge of riparian evergreen forest near Msondole in the Namizimu F.R. **p. 428**
De, Mj	Bb, Gs	**p. 428**
Ka	Ac, Gl	*See page 28.*
	Gl, Ma	**p. 426**
Lc, Cd	Gs, Gw	Often in flocks of over 50 birds. **p. 426**
Ld, Cd	Gs	May be found on short grass after burning. **p. 424**
Ld, Be	Dw	Common in the dambos between Dedza and Lilongwe. **p. 424**
	Gl	**p. 430**
Dz, De	Br, Th, Gl	In rank growth on the edge of riparian evergreen forest. **p. 430**
Ld, Bd	Th	Congregates in flocks when bamboos seed. **p. 430**
Mp, Sv	Ac, Gs	Often on bare ground. **p. 428**
Dz, Mj	Br	This and the next species may sometimes be found together. **p. 442**
Dz	Ac, Mo, Br	Usually in drier areas than the Cabanis's Bunting. **p. 442**
	Br, Ac	Prefers stony ground in light woodland. **p. 442**
De, Mj	Ro	Favours areas of large boulders. **p. 442**
	Br, Mo, Ac	**p. 436**
Sv	Ac	Confined to the lower Shire valley. **p. 440**
	Br, Ac, Bb	Often alongside the Yelloweyed Canary but less common; prefers more often country. **p. 436**

BOM	Family / species	Stat.	Al.	Ra.	Nat. Park
615	Cape Canary *S. canicollis*	ULRe	H	N	N – – –
616	African Citril *S. citrinelloides*	F/Re	HM	T	N – – –
617	Streaky Canary (Seedeater) S. *striolatus*	U/Re	H	N	N – – –
618	Stripebreasted Canary (Seedeater) *S. reichardi*	F/Re	HM	T	N K – –
619	Blackeared Canary *S. mennelli*		F/Re	M	T N K –
620	Oriole Finch *Linurgus olivaceus*	RLRe	HM	N	N – – –

Local.	Habitat	Comments
Mi, Vi	Bb, Gs	Only north of the Viphya Plateau above 1 800 m. **p. 436**
De, Mj	Br, Bb	*See page 28.*
Vi	Bb, Gl	*See page 28.*
Dz, De	Br	*See page 28.*
Dz, Ph	Br, Gl	**p. 438**
Mi	Ef	*See page 28.*

INDEX TO SCIENTIFIC NAMES

104

INDEX TO ENGLISH NAMES